Praise for Tim Chaney's
HOW MUCH FREEDOM SERIES

"In Tim Chaney's *How Much Freedom* series, he so eloquently brings home the new recipe for more freedom in our lives. And what's most exciting is that you don't have to travel far and wide to get it, or achieve next to impossible feats to find it. In this remarkable read, Tim shows us how to kick the doors wide open to live more freely, right here, right now."

Allison Maslan, Author of *Blast Off! The Surefire Success Plan to Launch Your Dreams into Reality*

~~~

"The *How Much Freedom* series provides a transformative opportunity for people seeking to unlock their full potential and experience deep fulfillment in their careers and personal lives. Reading these books is like a conversation with a wise friend – enjoyable and full of insight. Anyone who feels they haven't achieved the success they deserve should read these books."

Emily Bardeen, Director,
University of Virginia Alumni Association Career Services

~~~

"Tim Chaney lays out an understanding of life, and the way we choose to live it that is, quite simply, life-altering. The *How Much Freedom* series is full of illustrations that teach us how living from the inside-out inevitably leads to freedom, happiness, and a sense of inner peace. It is astonishing to realize that such a simple approach can have such a dramatic impact on our everyday lives."

Carrie Nixon, Esquire,
Chief Executive Officer of Nixon Law Group

"The *How Much Freedom* series will inspire, challenge, and energize you, but most importantly, it will transform your experience. Your life will simply never be the same again. Tim beautifully illustrates how chasing after achievements frequently leads to disillusionment and disappointment and deftly shows you how to create a new experience in any moment by focusing on true success from the inside-out. Tim guides readers towards discovering the power they hold within themselves, and through thoughtful and effective examples, illuminates how each of us can leverage our inner wisdom and transform our lives in an instant. These books will help you create the life you want and be authentically happy doing it. Do yourself a favor and read them now!"

Elisa Canova, Managing Partner,
The Artemis Group Consulting, LLC

~~~

"Tim does a masterful job of navigating the reader through some simple, yet incredibly powerful principles. There is so much for a reader to hook onto to live life differently and effortlessly starting right now. The *How Much Freedom* series is a gift to every reader to live the great life they want, recognizing they have everything they need within themselves to do just that."

Jeannette Lichner, Senior Managing Director at FTI Consulting, author of *#yourmoney: Everything You Need to Know About Earning, Spending, and Saving*, and Executive and Young Person's Coach

~~~

"The *How Much Freedom* series is fantastic! I experienced wonderful insights as I read it. If you're looking for a book to help you get to the next level, this incredible read clearly stands out from the crowd."

Anna Reynolds, Performance Coach

"If ever you were looking for something to demonstrate the clear connection between state of mind, quality of thought, and results, you have found it. Gently stripping away, page after page, any last need for struggle, anxiety, or resistance, Tim's whole series is a testament to the title of the first book: truly, *How Much Freedom Can You Stand?*"

David Firth, Author of *Change Your World One Word at a Time* and *From Making a Living to Creating a Life*

~~~

"Most people never get the shot that this book gives its lucky reader ... a fresh shot at freedom and success without stress or strain. Buy this book now."

Steve Chandler, Author of *Wealth Warrior: The Personal Prosperity Revolution* and *Time Warrior: How to Defeat Procrastination, People-pleasing, Self-doubt, Over-commitment, Broken Promises and Chaos*

How Much

FREEDOM

Can You Stand?

How Much

FREEDOM

Can You Stand?

The Stress-free Way
to
Live the Life You Really Want

TIM CHANEY

Success Partnerships

Published by Success Partnerships
Charlottesville, VA

Cover and Interior Art by Sarah Courtney Glenn
Edited by Julie Blake & Monica Chaney
Author Photo by Carolyn Watson Photography

The author of this book does not dispense medical advice or prescribe the use of any technique as a form of treatment for physical, emotional, or medical problems without the advice of a physician, either directly or indirectly. The intent of the author is only to offer information of a general nature to help you in your quest for emotional and spiritual well-being. In the event you use any of the information in this book for yourself, the author and publisher assumes no responsibility for your actions.

Tim Chaney's website:
www.freedomfirstliving.com

First Edition

Printed in the United States of America

ISBN: 978-0-9915238-0-1 (s)
ISBN: 978-0-9915238-2-5 (e)
ISBN: 978-0-9915238-1-8 (m)

To my beautiful wife, Monica - you are my best friend, the love of my life, and the inspiration for all that I do. This book would not be possible without you.

To my amazing son, Drew - your ability to follow your inner promptings every day is one of the big reasons why I'm finally doing work that I love to do. I'm deeply honored to be your Dad.

The How Much Freedom Series

Book 1
How Much Freedom Can You Stand?
The Stress-free Way to Live the Life You Really Want

Book 2
How Much Freedom Are You Missing?
The Stress-free Way to Overcome Every Challenge

Book 3
How Much Freedom Can You Create?
The Stress-free Way to Succeed on Your Own Terms

Contents

Acknowledgments

Any time you embark on a significant project like writing a book, there are always countless people whose support and assistance make the whole thing possible. I want to acknowledge the individuals who have had the most direct impact on helping me bring this work to completion. There are so many people whose contribution to my life made this work possible that I cannot possibly acknowledge them all.

First, I want to express my deepest gratitude to my beautiful wife, Monica. She is my best friend, the love of my life, my soul mate, my biggest supporter, and my editor. Her contributions made my manuscript worthy of publication.

Next, I want to thank my son, Drew, for being my greatest teacher. He continually inspires me and shows me how precious life is. Seeing the world through his eyes has awakened a part of me that was previously dormant. This book and my work would simply not be possible without him.

Don Chaney, my father, who was taken from this earth far too soon, taught me to dream big and live every day to the fullest.

Linda Chaney, my mother, who sacrificed so much to give me the best opportunities in my childhood and who always saw great possibilities for me.

Michael Neill, the best coach on the planet and a phenomenal mentor, for teaching me what great coaching looks like.

Steve Chandler for his life-changing distinctions and showing me the value of action in creating your reality.

George Pransky whose teaching of the Three Principles created the greatest transformation in my life and now forms the foundation for my work.

Garret Kramer and Mara Gleason, two esteemed colleagues in the Three Principles community whose work I deeply respect, for sharing honest insights about my manuscript and challenging me to take it to another level.

Julie Blake, my co-editor and creative collaborator, who helped transform the power of my words to impact the readers I most deeply want to help.

Sarah Courtney Glenn, the artistic genius whose work graces the cover of this book and who has patiently listened to my half-formed ideas and somehow turned them into something beautiful.

Yvenne King, whose expert legal guidance saved me a great deal of consternation.

I want to thank my clients for inspiring me and pushing me to new heights. Thank you all!

Preface

Welcome to the first book in the How Much Freedom series, *How Much Freedom Can You Stand*.

When I sat down to write *How Much Freedom Can You Stand* three years ago, I never envisioned having so much to say. Although I was stunned, my wife was not nearly as surprised.

When I saw the proofs for the final manuscript, it became crystal-clear to me that this book needed to be divided into more consumable chunks. I want you, the reader, to easily integrate what I'm sharing here. I want you to enjoy happiness and peace of mind no matter what's happening around you. I want you to be able to pause and really reflect on each installment.

So, I decided to release this manuscript as three distinct books. Each really does stand on its own and gives you the chance to make a quantum leap forward in the freedom you experience.

As an author, the most important thing for me was always this -- that readers' lives were significantly transformed, and that they got better results. Not marginally better. Off-the-charts better.

If you were to read only one book in the series, *How Much Freedom Can You Stand* would be the book to read. This book will show you how to live the life you really want, without stress.

Book 2, *How Much Freedom Are You Missing*, will be released in late summer of 2015. It debunks the 11 commonly-held beliefs about what it takes to be successful. Whether you're already succeeding or working hard to finally break through, one or more of these beliefs is undoubtedly holding you back. After reading Book 2, you'll know with certainty what really leads to extraordinary success and how to use it to get results like never before.

Book 3, *How Much Freedom Can You Create*, will be released in late 2015. It will show you how to succeed with ease -- without stress, pressure, striving, or force of will. If you have a burning desire to succeed wildly on your own terms while maintaining a balanced life, this is the book for you.

Reading through the Introduction and What's Next sections of the manuscript, I felt strongly that they both work well with each of the three books. Also, I wanted to make sure that no reader misses out on these important sections because they found Book 2 or Book 3 first. That's why I opted to repeat these two sections in all three books.

Similarly, because the testimonials at the beginning of the book were written based on the full manuscript, I decided to print them in each of the three books as well.

I am deeply grateful that you've purchased this book. It is my sincere hope that it will help you live completely free, where stress is a distant memory and success is a frequent companion.

To Your Freedom and Success,

Tim Chaney
Charlottesville, VA
February, 2014

Introduction

Freedom -- it's what most of us spend our entire adult lives chasing. We work hard and long. We spend time away from our families. We travel. We tolerate bad bosses. We endure stress. We compromise our dreams. All in the hopes that someday, we'll achieve enough to finally be free to live the life we really want.

But is that the best strategy? It largely depends on what freedom looks like to you.

- When you think of freedom, do you think of leaving a less-than-satisfying job and sailing off into the sunset?

- Do you dream of retiring from a 40-year career and doing whatever you want 24/7?

- Do you imagine never again answering to a demanding boss, working weekends, or being on-call?

Almost without fail, when you talk to people about freedom, what they describe is a destination...something outside of themselves...something that they must strive to attain. If freedom seems like an elusive place to you, one that if you could somehow reach it, would bring all the happiness, joy, and fulfillment you've always dreamed about, then you've got it all backwards.

Which would you prefer,

A) Pushing and willing yourself toward a far-off finish line in the hopes that you'll have enough left at the end of the race to enjoy the victory?

OR

B) Running freely every step of the way with a lightness and effortlessness that is so fun that you enjoy every moment, and consequently you are so surprised when you cross the finish line that it doesn't even occur to you to stop?

Pursuing freedom by acquiring enough material success so you own your time is one way to go about it. If you're one of the elite few who actually get there with your health, relationships, and vitality in tact, maybe it's worth it.

But if all of us are chasing freedom this way, why don't more of us have it? Could it be that we're looking in the wrong place? Could it be that we're starting the chase from a fundamentally flawed premise?

Are you willing to wait for **SOMEDAY** to live the life you really want to be living?

Running on Empty

If you were planning a once-in-a-lifetime, cross-country trip, would you set out with your oil gauge pointing at LOW?

Obviously, that would be foolish. Running on low oil can lead to costly repairs and in some cases, may completely destroy the engine. Why would you want to risk such an important trip by operating from a flawed foundation? Yet, there's a good possibility you're doing exactly that in your own life.

Let me ask you something. Are you a high achiever -- someone who wants to accomplish big things and pushes yourself really hard to do better and do more? Do you want to make a big difference in the world and leave a lasting legacy? Does it often feel like a struggle?

Or perhaps, you're not even struggling, you're just wondering if there's a better way to create the results you're striving for. Pause and reflect for a few seconds. Do any of these questions resonate with you?

- Does it feel like you're running on a really fast treadmill and one misstep will sending you flying?

- Is your mind so busy you have trouble really relaxing and enjoying yourself?

- Is there something significant you want to create that's not happening as quickly as you'd like?

- Despite working so hard to produce great results, do you still feel like something is missing?

For so many people, the pathway to a life of fulfillment, success, and happiness is a struggle. Sometimes it feels like the success you want so badly depends on achieving certain results, and they're just not happening. The harder you think, the more elusive the answers seem to become.

Other times it feels like you're working really hard and realizing success, but you're neither happy nor fulfilled. The success in one area of life seems to come at the expense of all the others. You suspect that the ensuing guilt and frustration are undermining your results and enjoyment.

Then there are times you feel like your stuck in a rut that you'll never break free from. The more you try to escape, the deeper you descend.

Fear not. If you are ready to experience more freedom than you have in a long time, and enjoy the fulfillment and success that inevitably comes with it, you have the right book in your hands.

Whether you're a high achiever in your profession, or you simply aspire to be, there is a much better approach to life. Despite what you have been conditioned to believe, creating and sustaining success is not inherently stressful. Actually, nothing is.

The circumstances of your life don't have to impact your ability to enjoy it. And when stress and struggle are no longer concerns, you'll get dramatically better results than you've ever gotten before.

Whether you are a CEO, an attorney, a corporate manager, a business owner, or anyone else for that matter, there is a:

- Fun, stress-free way to produce unprecedented results

- New understanding that will allow you to relax no matter what's happening in your life or in your head

- Simplicity to life that will be yours when your mind is free

Is it really possible to live virtually stress-free, with a deep sense of inner peace and happiness, and still create the success you want? The answer as you'll see in this book is a resounding, "YES!!!"

But it won't happen by doing things differently. It won't happen by becoming someone different. It won't happen by trying to think better thoughts.

Those all require lots of work and self-discipline. If they actually worked more often, I might endorse them. If you're like me, you want happiness, fulfillment, and success, **AND YOU WANT TO HAVE FUN CREATING THEM! AND YOU DON'T WANT TO WAIT TO HAVE THEM.**

To create unprecedented results and have fun doing it, freedom must come first. The good news is Kid Rock's not the only one who was born free[1]. We all have access to freedom in any moment, and that access is available without hard work, mental toughness, or willpower.

All that's required is a new understanding of how your experience of life is actually created. By the time you finish this book, you'll be seeing your world in ways you never have before, and your experience will be forever transformed.

A Magic Little Pill

What if I told you there was an all-natural magic pill you could take that would give you all the freedom you've been striving for? The pill has no side effects whatsoever. You don't need to change your diet or your lifestyle in any way for the pill to be effective. In fact, making those changes is discouraged. When you use the magic pill regularly, you will:

- Consistently produce innovative, creative ideas
- Dramatically increase your energy and ability to focus, so your productivity soars
- Minimize your lows and maximize the highs, so you get unprecedented results
- Perform at your best, regardless of circumstance, any time you want
- Permanently eliminate the need for any strategies, techniques, or coping mechanisms
- Bounce back from setbacks with ease and grace
- No longer have to try so hard
- Experience little or no stress
- See marked improvement in every aspect of your life

Would you take it? Well, there's actually no such magic pill. But there is an understanding about life that's just as simple and just as powerful as any drug you could take. And there is a very, very good chance you've never heard it before. Until now!

If you've ever dreamed of calling your own shots in life and doing lucrative, soul-fulfilling work, accomplishing a seemingly impossible feat, or simply living a life where every day is a new, exciting adventure, this is the book for you.

This revolutionary understanding is what I call Freedom First Living. It's the foundation for unparalleled innovation, high productivity, peak performance, and extraordinary resilience. It's the foundation for stress-free living, happiness, and fulfillment. It's the basis for great ideas and great work.

So... if there is an understanding that's so life-changing, why haven't you heard about it before?

It's All Just A Big Misunderstanding

What if you were invited to a party at a fancy hotel, and you were super excited to go. You got dressed to the nines, hired a sitter, and just for fun, you took a few dance lessons so you could make a big splash. As you rushed out the door, you grabbed your invitation with the directions on the back. Only when you arrived at the hotel, there was no sign of a party. Turns out, there was a typo in the directions, and now here you sit, completely lost!

Meanwhile, just a couple of blocks away, in a similar hotel, the party is in full swing. The band is playing. The partygoers are dancing and having a grand time. Vibrant energy fills the room. The only thing missing is you!

I DON'T WANT YOU TO MISS OUT ON THE REAL PARTY -- YOUR WONDERFUL LIFE!

This book gives you precise directions to the party, and once you have them, you'll never be lost again.

It's Easier than You've Ever Imagined

The truth is the only reason most of us aren't living the life we really want is because we've been given some misinformation, not unlike the typo on the invitation. That misinformation costs us peace of mind, creativity, happiness, and freedom. That misinformation is all that separates us from consistently performing our best - even when our thinking isn't perfect. As I've come to discover, **you will stop being so concerned with what**

you think when you see how little consequence it has on who you are and what you can become.

Almost everything we've been taught about life is backward. It wasn't done out of maliciousness or intent to deceive. It was an innocent mistake. But it was a significant mistake nonetheless.

You see, I have spent most of my adult life desperately searching to find my life's work. I was on a quest to find joy, passion, fulfillment and, yes, freedom -- the freedom to run my own successful company and earn a great living doing something I loved.

My dream has always been to be an entrepreneur. To call the shots in my life. To live life solely on my terms. To create something uniquely mine. And to make an enormous difference in the lives of others while doing it.

I've spent more time studying, reading, and learning ways to create success than you can imagine. If you're like me, you've probably spent countless hours in the bookstore as well, reading works from the Business Section, the Spiritual/Personal Development Section, and the Money/Finance Section. You're constantly looking for ways to improve yourself. You're adding knowledge, skills, and new ideas to your repertoire.

For the past 15 years, that's been my modus operandi. In an effort to find happiness and success, I studied and applied positive thinking, affirmations, meditation, hypnosis, time management, retirement planning, positive psychology, mental toughness and many other strategies and approaches. There are countless others that I didn't bother trying because they seemed like too much work. The ones I tried helped some, yet the life I longed for seemed just as elusive as ever.

I've even tried things that are, well, out there. Once, back in the 90s, I even did a fire walk. That's right, I walked across a bed of scorching hot coals. The purpose of things like fire walks, I suppose, is for people to prove to themselves that fear can be overcome. That you can do anything. It's meant to be a life-changing experience. You know what I discovered?

I discovered that I can walk across hot coals. That's it! Do you think that experience eliminated or reduced my fear in other areas of my life? Not one iota. The impact on my life lasted about as long as the few blisters on the bottom of my feet.

If my life were a game of Monopoly, I was moving forward one space at a time, not accumulating much property, and slowly running out of funds. Then, I came across something so different...so profound...so simple...and so life-changing that it was as if I instantly had hotels on every property, owned all 4 railroads, and held all the money in the bank.

I had learned the best-kept secret in personal development, human performance, and business all rolled into one. How had this information escaped my radar for 15 years? Why weren't more people teaching this understanding?

There are more business and thought leaders today than ever before. With the proliferation of blogs, podcasts, and other forms of social media, there is no shortage of experts on how to improve your business and your life. For the most part, they all want to make a difference. Their hearts are in the right place, and they're teaching the best of what they know.

Unfortunately, most of the advice is not useful. Not because it isn't sound or didn't work for the advisor. But because without a deeper understanding of what's behind the human experience, you'll struggle to apply that advice. When it doesn't work as well for you, you're in a bind. Is the problem with the advice or with you? That's the dilemma I wrestled with time and time again for most of those 15 years.

Prior to this new understanding, I struggled mightily. I hated my career more than supermodels hate carbs. I had no clue what I wanted to do with my life other than to be free. Luckily, I had an incredibly happy marriage to my best friend and love of my life.

She supported me through these challenging times, and her love buoyed my hopes that someday I'd find my calling.

Back in 2010, I enrolled in an elite coach-training program to learn from arguably the best coach practicing today. His name is Michael Neill. What made Michael's program unique is rather than teach everything himself, he brought in his own mentors to facilitate. In six live weekends, a different teacher shared the stage with Michael to share extraordinary wisdom and help us hone our craft.

In addition, Michael brought another dozen teachers to share their methodologies through "virtual master classes," 90-minute teleseminars, designed to impart new coaching frameworks to add to our toolbox. All of those teachers were outstanding and entertaining. But there was one masterclass that impacted me most.

Dr. George Pransky, a PhD psychologist from LaConner, Washington, presented information that was radically different from anything I'd heard before. At first, quite honestly, I was thoroughly confused. I didn't grasp much of what George was saying but somehow I knew what he was sharing was significant. I couldn't get it out of my head.

You see, George had a similar experience learning from author and philosopher, Sydney Banks[2]. Banks's insights about the fundamental principles that are core to the human experience have come to be known as the Three Principles: Mind, Consciousness, and Thought.

Syd's epiphanies about life and his subsequent teachings so profoundly influenced Pransky that he essentially dropped everything he had learned about practicing therapy and focused solely on helping people through this new understanding. And the results have been extraordinary.

When Dr. Pransky made some of his audio programs available to us, I took advantage. I took them with me to the gym. I listened and listened and listened some more. Little by little I started to see things from a fresh perspective. As Michael began to evolve his work, I noticed the new way he coached others on his radio show, and I was hooked. I continued learning and absorbing all that I could about this new understanding...what I now refer to as Freedom First Living.

Then one day I had one of those "lightbulb moments," and everything changed. My circumstances hadn't changed at all, yet everything seemed different. I finally understood the key to stress-free living, confidence, high performance, creativity, and producing extraordinary results.

How in 15 years had I not come across this understanding? I'd read all the well-known experts. None of them had this understanding of life. In fact, what they were teaching was just plain inaccurate.

It was an innocent mistake with profound implications. As I looked around, I saw that almost everyone I knew was living with the same fundamental misunderstanding. It was robbing them of joy, peace of mind, fun, and the results they really wanted. Once I saw this, my life's work was no longer a mystery.

Free Your Mind, Results Will Follow

My goal is to change your life right now. I don't want you to waste 15 years or even 15 minutes waiting to live the life you really want. I want you to be free starting right now.

This book will show you how. How long will it take? That's hard to say. Clients who work with me privately typically see a profound reduction in stress within the first few weeks, and a significant transformation in the results they're producing within 4-6 months. Sometimes it takes longer but the truth is, it can happen in an instant. All that's required is seeing the truth about how life really works.

The best part about my clients' experience is that even if our work is focused on one area of their life, all of the other areas improve. And they sustain these results because, unlike strategies, techniques, and advice, personal understanding is permanent. Once you see something new, you don't un-see it.

What will it take for your life to transform?

It will require an open mind. It will require you to look in directions you've never looked before. Yes, it will even require you to drop some of your most cherished beliefs.

It won't involve hard work; in fact, it's effortless. There's nothing to practice. No discipline is required. You won't need to *become a warrior, a buddha, or a Pollyanna*. It doesn't matter what you think - positive or negative. All that's needed is a willingness to look inward and see what's really going on.

I don't meditate, say affirmations, practice yoga regularly, use mindfulness, chant or do anything else to alleviate or manage stress. Not that there's anything wrong with those things! If you love them, fantastic! Use them. Just know this -- they're absolutely unnecessary to live a happy, stress-free life.

Here's what I mean. Yoga, meditation, and other practices cannot take away stress, although it looks for all the world like they can. There's something else at play. In this book you'll discover why things like yoga, exercise, meditation, and deep breathing appear to reduce stress. And it's that understanding that's the real game-changer.

The capacity to create the extraordinary resides not in hard work, thinking hard, or pushing yourself more. It arises from spending more and more time connected to your deeper intelligence -- the intelligence that provides an endless stream of insight and innovative solutions.

Does that mean you can sit cross-legged on the floor, staring at your Vision Board, chanting, and affirming, "I will succeed. I will succeed," and results will magically happen?

It's doubtful. There will be things to do and actions to take, but it won't feel like work, and it won't require motivation and pushing yourself.

You may find that you become increasingly aware of your own thinking. At first, you'll likely think more about your thinking than before. Questions and confusion may arise. For a time, your mind may get noisier. This is quite common. At this stage, many clients wonder what they should do to make the thinking quiet down.

The answer is nothing. Think of it like this. If you've ever learned to play an instrument or speak a new language, at first, playing or speaking is mechanical and awkward. You have to think about what you're doing. That thinking impacts your ability to perform smoothly. Eventually if you keep playing or speaking, the thinking quiets down. Pretty soon, you're playing or speaking without thinking at all. Playing and speaking have become second nature.

The same is true with your ability to know when to let certain thoughts go without further investment. As you see the truth about the way you experience life, it will be second nature for you to operate with a free mind. And a free mind is the ultimate performance enhancer.

I want you to live life with a completely free mind because I know if you do, you'll live the life you really want.

This book is designed to impart this radical, new understanding to you. Together, we'll take a look at how life really works. We'll learn how human beings thrive. We'll explore the real secrets to lasting happiness, peace of mind, creativity, and extraordinary performance.

We'll destroy commonly-held ideas that are mainstays of most coaching methodologies. We'll obliterate common myths about what holds you back.

Are you struggling with one or more of the issues on this list?

- Lack of confidence
- Self-sabotage
- Setting goals improperly or not at all
- Fear
- Lack of motivation
- Lack of time
- Inability to live up to expectations
- Lack of mental toughness
- Procrastination
- Unwillingness to take risks
- Lack of commitment

As it turns out, all the things that look like bona fide obstacles to success are merely illusions. Your ability to see beyond the illusion is what enables you to move past them with more grace and velocity.

Simply put, if you believe your struggles have to do with any of the things listed above, you're not seeing clearly. There is something common to all of these maladies, and once you see this common thread, you'll be free from these nasty mind viruses once-and-for-all.

One Thought Away

Believe it or not, we'll do this without step-by-step formulas, strategies, or techniques. We'll do it without positive thinking, affirmations, or reframing. We'll do it without mental toughness.

So how will we do it?

Imagine you and I are on a birdwatching trip. Suddenly, I spot one of the birds we've both been eager to see - the Painted Bunting. It's arguably the most colorful bird in North America, and I've got it squarely in the lens of my binoculars. This is the holy grail of birds for both of us; the one we desperately wanted to see on this trip.

I really want you to see this little beauty, so I start giving you instructions for where to point your binoculars so you'll see the bird. First, I say, "Look out toward the water. Do you see the Live Oak tree to the left of the big palm? Look up toward the top of the Live Oak at about 11 o'clock."

As you keep scanning the tree with your binoculars, I describe the branch the bunting is perched on. "You see the branch that makes a "Y" shape? Look behind that to the left. See the brownish leaf that looks like a ghost? Look slightly to the right and behind that. You should be able to see his striking blue head peeking out."

Finally, your binoculars lock onto the bird. You are in awe. You've never seen anything so spectacular. The combination of blue, red, yellow, and green is like nothing you've ever seen. Now that you have the bird in your binoculars, keeping him in your sights is easy.

This book will be much like the birdwatching trip in that each chapter is a new set of instructions to help you see this deeper understanding. I will repeat some of these ideas in slightly different ways. I will explore these ideas in different contexts. My only intent is straightforward - for you to see what I've seen. Consequently, my job is to keep pointing until you see for yourself.

I'm confident that once you see it, your life will never be the same. Stress will fall away. New insights and creative ideas will emerge. When issues arise, which they inevitably will, you'll take them in stride. Your circumstances and thinking will become inconsequential to producing the results you want. In short, you'll thrive in any and every circumstance you encounter from this day forward.

No matter what has happened in your life, no matter where you are now in relation to where you'd ultimately like to be, you're always only one thought away from total freedom.

Freedom Inquiry

To deepen your understanding and self-awareness, I invite you to engage with one or two thought-provoking questions at the end of each chapter. I call this Freedom Inquiry. These questions are designed to give you deeper insights into your own experience. Rather than answer each question as though you're taking a final exam, reflect on it. Sit with it. Or take it out on a long walk with you.

Don't rush. Allow answers to come to you without trying so hard. Resist the urge to censor yourself.

You may want to get a journal specifically for your inquiry and return to it from time to time. There is no right way to do this. You will get the most benefit by embracing the process fully.

The Ultimate Performance Breakthrough

If you're up to something big in your life, you may have already discovered that looking to the world of form for validation, confirmation, and evidence about what you should or shouldn't do is a significant mistake. You may have heard that the answers lie within. Perhaps you've come across seemingly sage advice like, "Thoughts become things, choose them wisely." So you conclude that what you think matters.

You recognize that self-defeating thoughts probably won't help you get where you're going, so you try to change your behavior or fix your thinking. You re-frame, say affirmations, develop mental toughness, and make commitments, all in the name of creating success. Success that you hope will lead to happiness, peace of mind, and a sense of fulfillment.

Everyone thinks. You are a thinking creature, and you pretty much think all the time. Given that, it makes sense that what you think and how you interpret those thoughts is paramount to your success and happiness, right?

The only limitation to living the life we really want is our own thinking. But not in the way you might think.

What if thoughts only appear to be things because you think they are? What if most of your thoughts show up whether you like it or not? What if what you think is actually irrelevant to your success?

I'm here to tell you that what you think is irrelevant. It's not the content of your thinking that matters. What matters is understanding the nature of thought, and the role state of mind and feelings play in shaping your experience.

Sydney Banks' personal insights represent perhaps the single-most transformative breakthrough in human well-being, psychology, and performance in history.

His insights provide the understanding that enables you to reliably create a clear mind and connect to deeper wisdom on a regular basis. They provide the lift for greater performance and creativity. Those insights have dramatically changed my life, and this book is my attempt to pass them along to you.

Would you attempt to build a house on a shaky foundation? I'm guessing you wouldn't. If you were lucky enough to succeed, you'd know that eventually the house would implode. With a firm foundation in place, however, you could build anything, from a log cabin to a beachfront condo, from a 40-room mansion to a 40-story office building, from a luxury hotel to an eco-friendly solar house.

Freedom First Living is the most stable (and fun!) foundation to build your life on. It's the understanding that makes creating anything possible. It's the platform for creating amazing results in your life. And you can do it all with a sense of ease and clarity so you won't:

- Let relationships suffer
- Sacrifice your health
- Waste time on projects that don't bring you joy
- Spend an enormous amount of time consumed with stress and worry

Once your mind is free, creating anything is a straightforward proposition. **Freedom is the starting block not the finish line.** With a clear, undistracted mind providing a steady wind in your sails, you will:

- Experience happiness, peace, and fulfillment at all time highs
- Produce significantly better results with less effort and struggle than you ever have.
- Leverage your time only on the most high value activities you actually enjoy
- Have way more fun "running the race," so that regardless of the outcome, you win (by the way, with far less pressure and emphasis on results, your results tend to be vastly superior)

If I'm Already Free, Won't I Stop Doing Stuff?

You may be asking yourself, "If I were happy and content all the time, wouldn't I lose the motivation and drive to succeed?"

Fair question. Turns out, you need not worry. I've been achievement-oriented my entire life. Whether it was academic achievement, athletic success, or wealth creation, as long as I can remember, I've had goals and dreams that I was working on.

As a high achiever, I tend to be a perfectionist. I want to do everything to the best of my ability, and I don't like settling for anything less. If you're a high achiever, you've probably noticed this yourself.

This achievement orientation rarely led to happiness or success I so desperately wanted, however. Short-lived euphoria, yes. Sustained happiness, not so much. The fun, stress-free approach that Freedom First Living offers has done nothing to diminish my desire to achieve. What it has done is help me navigate through life with much greater effectiveness. I understand what causes me to feel the way I do, so I don't waste precious time and energy trying to fix problems that don't really exist. These insights have been priceless to me.

As a high achiever, one of your biggest strengths may also be your Achilles' heel. Your intellect has served you well, so the idea that your thinking may not always be useful can be tough to swallow. Not always trying to figure things out may seem counter-intuitive. But the rational mind doesn't reveal the Truth as we assume it does. The richness and juiciness that you crave is sitting there waiting to serve you in the form of your own inner guidance. All you have to do is pull up a chair and join the party!

For the duration of this book, I would like for you to open up to the possibility that you don't have to figure everything out. Consider the notion that the beliefs you've held up until now are what will keep you from reaching the next level. If you are willing to suspend what you know, there is a very good chance that your life will expand in ways you never imagined were possible.

You are powerful beyond measure. You have everything inside you to create the life of your dreams. No matter where you are in your life or where you've been, you have the potential to create something extraordinary. There is no better time than right now to get started.

Here's the bottom line: you have the capacity to create anything your heart desires and your mind can imagine. The only things that ever hold you back are mirages. No matter how real they look to you, they are not real. This book will show you how to see beyond the illusion, so that your life is filled with miracles rather than problems.

One last thing -- while this book is written to benefit everyone, I'm deeply committed to helping women entrepreneurs and business leaders because I believe they have extraordinary gifts to share that have the power to heal our planet.

If you're a woman who has created a high level of success the traditional way and want to make an even bigger difference, but without the stress, pressure, long hours, and sacrifice you're accustomed to, this book is for you.

If you're a woman who knows deep in your heart that you have greatness inside, but you're struggling because you're trying to follow someone else's blueprint, not yours, this book is for you too.

I want you to thrive in every area of life. It's not only possible, it's inevitable now that you have this book in your hands.

Let us begin...

Author's Note: Throughout the book, I share stories of work I have done with clients over the past several years. I have changed their names and certain details to protect their privacy.

"A man who as a physical being is always turned toward the outside, thinking that his happiness lies outside him, finally turns inward and discovers that the source is within him."

- Soren Kierkegaard

Chapter 1

How Much Freedom
Can You Stand?

The Freedom Within

Once upon a time there was a little bird who lived in a suburban home with his owners. The little bird lived in a cage that hung from the kitchen ceiling, where he could watch the other birds frolic and forage through the window.

Most days when he watched the free birds, the caged bird felt jealous of how they could fly anywhere, eating whenever they wanted, and see far away places that he'd only be able to dream about.

The caged bird spent countless hours wondering if he would ever be free again. He longed to feel the warmth of the sun, the crispness of a winter morn, and the thrill of being able to look down at the landscape from high among the clouds.

Day after day, he pondered how to be free. He knew that the door to his cage was his ticket to freedom but he couldn't seem to figure out how to get his owner to leave it open. The more he tried to figure out a solution, the worse he felt. As time went by, his discouragement grew and grew. There were times when he didn't even bother to eat, he felt so low.

Before long, he had given up. The joy he used to get from fantasizing about joining the other birds was gone. "It's hopeless," he assumed.

Then one day, when his owner was away on vacation, a new boy came to take care of him. As soon as he saw the little caged bird, a look of sadness came over him. "Birds are meant to fly free, not to be locked in a cage," he muttered to himself.

The boy turned to open the window and then the door to the cage. Alas, here was the big chance the little caged bird was waiting for. He burst through the door and alit on the sill. Just as he was about to flee, a thought occurred to him.

"What if I don't make it in the real world? What if I'm safer here in the cage? What if freedom isn't all I've made it out to be?"

In that instant, the fear overwhelmed him, and he turned and zipped back into the cage - to the boy's astonishment.

Every day, the boy came and opened the window, followed by the cage door, hoping against hope that the little bird would find the courage to escape.

On the last day before the owner was due to return, the boy went through his usual ritual, but without the sense of conviction he had on the first day. There was a profound sadness in his heart. He couldn't bear to watch the freest of creatures trapped in a worthless cage. After all, the little bird had barely eaten all week.

By now, the boy had given up on the bird flying free so he didn't even bother to open the door this time. "The bird has been caged too long," he presumed.

As the boy tidied up, the little bird watched him and wondered, "Why does he want me to be free? What does he see that I don't?"

Then he noticed something he hadn't noticed before. Here was this boy walking freely around the house, and he was miserable. Suddenly, a realization hit the little bird. He wondered how he hadn't seen it before. "If a boy can walk around freely, and be miserable, then my misery can't be caused by this cage."

3

The bird felt happier than he had in a long time.

"I'm already free!! I've always been free - it's only when I've thought I wasn't that I felt caged. The cage itself can't take away my freedom. How could it?"

The bird was so delighted that he hopped over to his food and began to eat.

Just then, the boy turned toward the cage. What he saw caused him to do a double-take. The little bird was eating, and somehow he looked different. He looked happy, if that's possible for a bird.

The boy rushed to the window and opened it as quickly as he could. Then he turned and opened the door to the cage one more time.

The bird took one look at the boy, and one look at the door. This time the fear that had stopped him the previous six days was gone. Secure in the knowledge that he was already free, it no longer made sense to live in such confined quarters. And with that, the bird flew out the window and was gone.

Which Comes First, Freedom or Success?

Does success lead to freedom or does freedom lead to success? Visiting the self-help section of any bookstore suggests that success must come first as you undoubtedly will see far more books written about success than freedom. People have been conditioned to believe that the way to win freedom is to achieve high levels of success. When you retire, if you have managed your investments well, then you can enjoy freedom. Freedom is something way out in the future that you can have one day if you work really hard, and you have a bit of luck along the way.

Most people do not feel free, and believe that in order to get freedom, they must first become successful. Consequently, they often make choices based on what they think will get them the most success, even if it means having a career or job they don't actually like, compromising their principles to some degree, or **postponing true enjoyment of life**. Despite the fact that people attempt this path, very few actually achieve success this way and far,

far fewer people become free. But this remains the most likely journey that people who want freedom will embark upon.

This book will shift that formula 180 degrees. What I love about the fable at the beginning of this chapter is that it reveals an important truth, that we live in an inside-out world. Freedom, well-being, happiness, and peace do not come from things outside of us. They are innate. **You were born free, and then you learned to feel trapped.** You learned that freedom was something outside of you that you get when you have enough money, time, possessions, and accomplishment.

Freedom can be yours right now. Why? Because freedom, the ultimate freedom, lies inside YOU in this moment and always. The only question is, **"Are you in touch with your freedom or disconnected from it?"**

For much of my life, I saw freedom as a destination. It was an elusive, desirable place where once I finally arrived, I would be able to do whatever I wanted whenever I felt like it. The funny thing is, as I relentlessly pursued the destination of freedom, I never felt more trapped. What I was completely oblivious to was the potential to experience freedom in every single moment.

What about you? Are you striving and working feverishly for the day in the distant future when you can finally be free? Do you ever **slow down** enough to question the way you are **using** your life?

The reason I titled this book, *How Much Freedom Can You Stand?*, is because I've come to see life from a whole new perspective. Unbeknownst to me, freedom was available to me in any and every moment. And in fact I had experienced freedom many times before and attributed it to things outside of me.

I could have been enjoying freedom (albeit a slightly different kind) in any moment of my choosing. This freedom could have been mine anytime I wanted regardless of where I worked, whether I worked, how much money I made, how much money I had accumulated, how much stress I felt, or any other circumstance.

Only I wasn't aware that such freedom existed. **I was under the false impression that freedom was somewhere to get to.** And that my arrival in this utopian paradise known as freedom would only happen after I created certain tangible results in my life.

I had it all *backward*. I have come to see that **the most powerful freedom is the ability to connect to your innate happiness, creativity, resourcefulness, peace of mind, and loving spirit in any circumstance or situation**.

This kind of freedom is not dependent on controlling what happens to you, but recognizing that whatever you think about these circumstances is just that -- **only a thought**. It is largely made up, and will only become your reality if you continue to invest in those thoughts. **Your investment in these thoughts determines how much (or how little) freedom you experience.**

What a revelation! I had no idea that my freedom was always available to me, just as it is to you.

When you begin looking inward, you will be looking in the direction of the truth about the human experience. The more you look, and the more you are willing to see, the more likely you will see the truth about the innate nature of freedom. And that freedom knows no limits.

But first, let's explore the myth that success leads to freedom - the Achievement Model.

The Achievement Model

The Achievement Model (see the diagram on page 8) is something we're all taught growing up, either explicitly or implicitly, and it starts with an erroneous assumption: we are not free. **So we pursue freedom by chasing after success.**

We look outside of ourselves for the answers. We strive and strive with the hope that one day, if we're lucky, work really hard, and achieve enough, we'll accumulate enough success to finally be free.

So we put the vast majority of our energy on achievement. What is achievement? Simply put, achievement is completing a goal or milestone. Achievement is measurable, and generally speaking, can be observed and agreed upon by others. For example, you receive your PhD, you win a mini-triathlon, you earn a $50K bonus. Those are achievements.

In the Achievement Model, success is supposed to come from more and more achievement which eventually leads to freedom and hopefully, happiness and fulfillment.

Have you ever noticed that more and more achievement does not always lead to happiness and fulfillment?

Does it sometimes feel like despite all the achievement, freedom is further away than ever?

Is it possible that more and more achievement just leads to a greater level of achievement?

When people buy into the Achievement Model, even after achieving a great deal, they often feel unfulfilled and lack inner peace. Then, they wrongly conclude that they need to achieve even more. The only question is, "**How much achievement is enough?**"

What we fail to recognize is that the Achievement Model represents an outside-in approach to life, and it's a game we can never truly win. This model assumes, just like the little bird in the fable, that there is a destination outside of you that will bring you freedom -- that there is an amount of achievement that will be enough. What happens when we discover, like the bird, that without access to the freedom inside of us, we can never feel free-- even when we finally reach our destination?

The Achievement Model

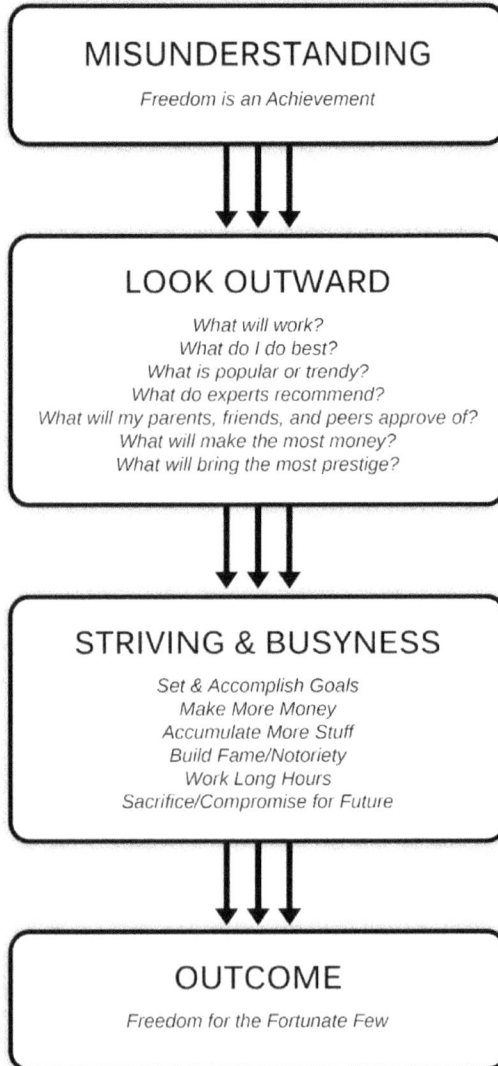

```
┌──────────────────────────────────────┐
│          MISUNDERSTANDING            │
│                                      │
│        Freedom is an Achievement     │
└──────────────────────────────────────┘
             │   │   │
             ▼   ▼   ▼
┌──────────────────────────────────────┐
│            LOOK OUTWARD              │
│                                      │
│           What will work?            │
│          What do I do best?          │
│       What is popular or trendy?     │
│      What do experts recommend?      │
│ What will my parents, friends, and peers approve of? │
│      What will make the most money?  │
│     What will bring the most prestige? │
└──────────────────────────────────────┘
             │   │   │
             ▼   ▼   ▼
┌──────────────────────────────────────┐
│         STRIVING & BUSYNESS          │
│                                      │
│        Set & Accomplish Goals        │
│           Make More Money            │
│        Accumulate More Stuff         │
│          Build Fame/Notoriety        │
│           Work Long Hours            │
│    Sacrifice/Compromise for Future   │
└──────────────────────────────────────┘
             │   │   │
             ▼   ▼   ▼
┌──────────────────────────────────────┐
│              OUTCOME                 │
│                                      │
│      Freedom for the Fortunate Few   │
└──────────────────────────────────────┘
```

What Is Freedom?

Most people view freedom as having enough wealth to do whatever you want whenever you want. This version defines freedom as a result and is far too narrow a definition. When people pursue the Achievement Model, they do not realize that there is a place inside them where real freedom exists. This is the insight that the little bird in the fable who chose to return to the cage had.

Freedom is a tremendous sense of peace, a knowing that no matter what happens in life, you will be okay.

Your happiness and enjoyment of life do not depend upon your bank balance, your real estate holdings, your marital status, or anything else outside of you. **The ultimate freedom comes from understanding where your experience of life originates, and how that experience can change in any moment, regardless of what is happening around you.**

When you are free, your sense of well-being does not fluctuate with the direction of the stock market or the world economy. When you experience complete Inner Freedom, your own thoughts do not exert control over you; you are able to recognize thought for what it is, and go about doing what you want to do regardless of what you're thinking.

Freedom is the recognition that you control very little of what goes on around you, but you have total control over your response.

But how do we know that achievement doesn't lead to freedom?

- There are politicians, Hollywood celebrities, and high profile athletes with millions of dollars who are not happy or secure, and fear they could lose it all.

- There are retired people with all the time in the world who are miserable and bored out of their minds.

- There are single people who struggle to make decisions even though they don't have to take another person's opinion into consideration.

What these people ultimately discover is that you cannot buy, win, or earn freedom because it's not *out there*. **Freedom is not a place to get to, freedom is a place to come from.**

Freedom is not the finish line. Freedom is the starting gate, and there is no finish line. There is nowhere you need to get to. You've already won the game.

Given that you've already won, you can keep playing by using your genuine desires as your means of navigation. You are free to experiment without your well-being at stake. That leads us to Freedom First Living.

Freedom First Living

Freedom is the foundation upon which you can create a wonderful, amazing life. It is the default state we all begin from. We start out with happiness, peace of mind and well-being. It's only when we get lost in our own thinking that we drift away. Yet no matter how far we've strayed, we always return to this fundamental state when we allow our thinking to pass. This fundamental state of well-being and peace is what I've termed Freedom First Living.

And as you begin living from Freedom First (see the diagram on page 12), you will create success on your terms. Success, then, is much different than achievement, and because it is self-defined, there is no formula for it. You live an authentic life based on your own definition of success, unaffected by circumstances, situations, other people, events, the world economy, and perhaps most importantly, your own thinking.

When people realize that freedom is theirs to experience whenever they choose, the things they choose to create will vary. Whatever form it happens to take is irrelevant if it is meaningful to you. For some people, it may be dating a supermodel, driving a

Porsche convertible, owning two mansions, and building a net worth in the millions. For others, it will be a loving family, a modest home, and enough money to take one vacation each summer. For others, it will be making a difference in the lives of the less fortunate.

When it is no longer a means to an end but simply a wonderful way to spend your life, you know you are free.

If you do not yet have material success, fear not. The irony when you live from Freedom First is that achievement is no longer an obsession. When your happiness, well-being, inner peace, and your very identity are no longer at stake based on what you do and what you accomplish, it becomes far easier to create the life you want. For one, what you choose to create is based on genuine wants, not what you think will lead to happiness, well-being, and inner peace. And since it stops being **so important**, it becomes easier to achieve.

FREEDOM FIRST LIVING

UNDERSTANDING

Freedom is our Natural State
(Happiness, Peace of Mind, Well-being)

LOOK INWARD

What would I love to do?
What feels right?
What would be fun?
What piques my curiosity?
What matters most to me?
How do I love to make a difference?

RICH EXPERIENCES

Innovative Ideas *Happier Relationships*
More Fun *Little or No Stress*
Greater Fulfillment *Freedom to Experiment*
Authentic Choices *Life on Your Own Terms*

OUTCOME

A Wonderful Life that You Absolutely Love

Freedom is not a place to get to.
It's a place to come from.

What if you find yourself in the same position as the bird in the fable sitting at the window listening to her sister's song? You have reached your desired destination (you have material success), but you still do not feel free. Now what? My invitation to you is to use this book to find your way back to the starting gate - your sense of well-being and peace. You don't have to return to the cage to find it. It is inside you, and you can discover it out on the windowsill and fly free!

Coming Up ...

Does it ever feel like happiness, security, and peace of mind are elusive things that you just can't seem to get enough of? In the next chapter, we will explore what it really means to lose your mind, and how to reconnect with your innate well-being at any time.

Freedom Inquiry

What impact has pursuing success via the Achievement Model had on your health? your relationships? your career? your inner peace? your results?

Chapter 2

Have You Lost
Your Mind?

Do you replay events in your mind, convinced that if you keep thinking about them, you'll eventually find a solution?

Do you try to control circumstances in order to create happiness, security, and prosperity?

Do you think worrying is productive?

Do you believe problems must be resolved?

Does it seem like what you're feeling is the direct result of what has happened to you?

Well, then you've lost your mind. Literally. When you're overthinking, trying to control things, worrying excessively, and believing that your feelings are caused by what happens to you, you've disconnected from your innate wisdom. **Fortunately, there is nothing you need to do to reconnect.** It will happen naturally when you stop trying to fix things in your head.

It will happen naturally when you stop replaying events in your mind and allow space to develop within your thinking. It is within this space that new, higher-level thinking emerges.

When you let go of the need to control everything in your world, either physically or mentally, you will be one step closer to freedom.

When you recognize that worrying has absolutely no value, you will be one step closer to freedom. People think that worrying keeps them safe. The truth is a worried mind is less responsive and more prone to mistakes and misinterpretation. You're less likely to accomplish anything productive in that state of mind. Although worrying sometimes looks like a better alternative than doing nothing, it never gets you anywhere either.

When you discover that you never have to solve a problem by figuring things out, that you can wait for a clear and cogent insight to create a breakthrough, you'll be even closer to freedom. The more you try to solve a problem by figuring things out, the more likely you'll never solve the problem. Instead, you will make the problem bigger and more daunting. Confusion is the by-product of an over-taxed mind.

When you understand that how you feel is always a result of how you interpret neutral events, you will be free.

The pathway to freedom is simple, yet often not easy to see. We are trained and rewarded for using our intellect. We worship the power of thinking, and while reasoning and logic are powerful tools, they are not tools to be used in every situation.

Hammers are great for pounding nails but not so good for drilling holes. Saws are great for cutting wood but not so good for measuring distances. The intellect is great for solving math problems and computing financial statistics but more often than you recognize, it is a poor choice for making career and business decisions, resolving relationship issues, and relieving stress and anxiety.

Your access to wisdom is unlimited, and it is your wisdom that has the capacity to solve any issue. The potential to accomplish anything you can imagine exists, and the path to that accomplishment resides in the wisdom you were born with, and that you can connect with at any time.

When you experience struggle, stress, conflict, indecision, anger, fear, despair, jealousy, confusion, or any negative emotion, you've lost your connection to deeper intelligence. The good news is that you don't need to do something extraordinary to reconnect. You simply have to stop the unnecessary spinning of thought and allow space for your wisdom to come through.

Over-thinking only accomplishes one thing -- it drowns out your wisdom.

What has helped me enormously is knowing that if I'm patient and don't get caught up in my own thinking, eventually incredible insights will appear in my consciousness. Working with my clients, I've seen over and over again that many times we already know what to do. Our wisdom is present, and if we look inward, we often know what it is telling us.

Recently, I had a session with a client named Shirley who has written a phenomenal memoir and wants to build a career as a motivational speaker. The problem was that her logical mind told her she didn't know how to do it. When we questioned the thought that she didn't know how, we discovered that it wasn't actually true. She in fact knew that the next step was to make some phone calls to organizations she'd love to present to. Her wisdom knew instantly that making proposals to speak was all she needed to do. The next bit of intellectual resistance came up around her fee. Within a minute, by tossing around potential speaking fees and asking if hers was higher or lower, she easily arrived at a fee she felt great about for now.

The answers were there all along, but she had temporarily cut off access to them by spending too much time thinking and not enough time listening.

You have all the wisdom you will ever need to accomplish anything you desire. It is available to you twenty-four hours per day, seven days per week. Even at your lowest moments, when you feel despondent and overwhelmed, stressed and scared, frustrated and angry, you never really lose your mind. You just momentarily disconnect from wisdom -- wisdom that is always there waiting to serve you.

Coming Up ...

Have you ever heard that happiness is a choice? Find out why that's not true, and what choice you *can* make that will lead to happiness 100% of the time.

Freedom Inquiry

How have intellect-based decisions helped you get to where you want to go? How have they prevented you from going further?

Chapter 3

The Pursuit of Un-Happiness

One of the things that seems to cause us the most unhappiness is our relentless pursuit of happiness. Pretty ironic, huh? I know for me that whenever I have experienced unhappiness in my life, it has led me to poor decision-making, unnecessary suffering, and less than satisfactory interactions with the people I love most.

Once I came to see that happiness is not something I could ever get from outside me, I realized why I had occasionally felt unhappy. I was looking for happiness in the wrong place. I was under the delusion that there was a pot of gold underneath a rainbow out there, and if I could somehow find it, I would be forever happy.

What never occurred to me was that I was not unhappy because I hadn't yet found the pot of gold, **I was unhappy because I deemed some less than happy thoughts as meaningful.**

The more I entertained those unhappy thoughts, the more convinced I was that I needed to find the pot of gold. Once I saw that it was just thought that was creating my experience of

18

unhappiness, I found it so much easier to **relax into the natural happiness that was always there.**

What's your pot of gold? Is it a seven-figure income, a paid-off mortgage, running your own business, making a living doing what you love, an incredible marriage? All of those are wonderful things, no doubt. But if you think the attainment of any or all of those things will make you happy, you are playing the game backwards.

Euphoria and Happiness

Recently, I identified a useful distinction between euphoria and happiness that may help you **relax into your own happiness**. I think that what so many of us, including myself, have been chasing is not happiness but euphoria.

Euphoria is a temporary surge of heightened joy and elation. It often shows up after an incredible meal, a promotion, winning a game in the last second, closing a big deal, falling in love, paying off your mortgage, or buying a new car. Euphoria is a wonderful feeling while it lasts, but it's not sustainable. Why not? Because it's not your natural state. When your mind is quiet, are you euphoric?

Euphoria is an illusory pot of gold.

Euphoria is not a bad thing -- if you recognize it for what it is. It's so easy to confuse the feelings of euphoria, the good feelings that rush in when something exciting happens, as happiness. Unfortunately, that confusion has major implications for your ability to enjoy your life.

It can lead to doing things you don't really want to in order to get more of those feelings. Pushing yourself harder believing that happiness is just around the corner. Sacrificing your health, relationships, and quite frankly, your life, searching for something that can never be found where you are looking.

Happiness, for me, is much different than euphoria. Happiness is much subtler. It is a state of well-being and contentment. It is the feeling that, "Life is good, and I'm okay just the way things are." When you are happy, you are not excited and jumping up and down with giddiness -- that's euphoria. When you are happy, you are relaxed and peaceful. You enjoy the simple things in life. You notice the birds, the flowers, and the laughter of children. Happiness is not something you get, it is who you are. **Happiness is your natural state when it is not being obscured by your attachment to your thinking.**

Happiness is the default. Euphoria is a gift, albeit a temporary one.

Happiness is a connection with the deepest part of yourself. And that connection is always available to you, in any moment, in any circumstance.

The only reason that connection ever breaks is when you fall under the illusory spell that what you think has meaning.

If you follow the bread crumbs of your thoughts, sometimes they lead you to believe you're unhappy. Sometimes they lead you to euphoria. But if
you notice the crumbs without necessarily following them, you will connect with your innate happiness.

Happiness is your natural state. If you're not feeling happy, it's only because you've gotten lost in the world of thought.

Think of it this way; there are days when the sun is obscured by the clouds. There are dark, gloomy, rainy days when it seems as though the sun does not exist. There are days when there are some clouds that occasionally drift in front of the sun, obscuring it temporarily until they drift further and reveal the golden rays once again. Then, there are bright, sunny days without a cloud in the sky. **Such is the nature of happiness, sometimes obscured but always present.** Knowing that the sun is always there, no matter how gloomy it may sometimes appear, all you ever have to do is wait. It will always return.

Is Happiness a Choice?

Recently I came across an excerpt from a book that really got my attention. The suggestion was made that happiness is a choice and that if you're committed enough to being happy, you will be. While I most definitely agreed with the author that circumstances do not determine our happiness, I don't see happiness as a choice in quite the same way as he suggests.

The design of human beings simply doesn't work that way. **We are thinking beings but we do not control the mechanism of thought.** Sometimes an unhappy thought will occur to us, and we will feel sadness. We certainly have a choice about what we do with the unhappy thought and how much more thought we add to it, but to suggest that we can always be happy if we commit to it is a fundamental misunderstanding of where happiness comes from.

No matter how committed I decide to be, I cannot prevent a sad thought from entering my consciousness. I would no longer be human if I could. So sometimes I'll feel happy, and sometimes I'll feel sad. And if I understand how the system works, I'll recognize that when sadness is present, there is nothing I need to do for happiness to return.

And it is that choice, the choice to allow the system to work naturally without interference, that you can always make.

Not long ago, I was hired by a client who was really struggling to find any happiness in her job. She wanted out-- and fast. She had risen to a fairly high level in the company, but her work no longer brought any fulfillment. She felt like her colleagues lacked integrity, and her position was tenuous at best.

She was torn between searching for a new job and creating a business of her own. Her confidence was clearly shaken by what was transpiring in her current role. In short, her viewpoint was severely limited and she was miserable.

Together, over several months we looked at the nature of thought, state of mind, and the human experience. Little by little, she began to see things from a much more neutral perspective. Options that previously seemed unavailable were now viable.

Then some interesting things began to happen. She was able to have conversations with her current management and create a better working environment for herself. She had fun looking at properties for a potential new business venture. To her big surprise, she was even able to find peace when visiting her in-laws.

Her calmer, more clear-seeing demeanor enabled her to avoid impulsive decisions and perform her best on job interviews. She turned down opportunities that were not good fits even though they might bring short-term relief.

She realized that the timing just didn't feel right for the business she really wanted to start. She was in tune with her wisdom much more often, and astute enough to ignore her unproductive thinking whenever it showed up.

Eventually, a great job offer came through; it was almost exactly what she was looking for. She'd be in charge of running a large team, mentoring younger staff, and she'd be challenged. She liked the people she'd be working with. The decision was simple and straightforward. As is so often the case, things that look like crises from a low state of mind, often turn out beautifully when we allow them to unfold naturally.

Do you need commitment to start a car's engine? Not if you know that placing the key in the ignition and turning it will do the job. The funny thing is, when you understand how the system works, you will experience far more happiness than you ever will trying to avoid sadness.

The Pot of Gold

If you are a high achiever, you may be thinking that happiness leads to complacency. I need a pot of gold to drive me, or I won't do anything. Relax! It's simply not true. What is it that you are driving yourself toward? What is your pot of gold? What will getting that pot of gold do for you?

If it's happiness or freedom you're looking for, stop looking. Both are available inside of you right now. As I have so delightfully discovered, I still have ambitions and desires, and I actually have more fun making them into reality because it doesn't seem to matter so much whether I actually succeed.

Coming Up ...

Have you unknowingly given over control of your life? If so, then your life is probably nowhere near what it could be. To get where you most want to go, distinguishing wisdom from the voice of your inner critic is critical.

In the next chapter, you'll discover one of the common ways that you're unwittingly disconnecting from the source of your best ideas, and the secret to detecting your wisdom so you can thrive.

Freedom Inquiry

What would you still want to accomplish if you were already happy and free?

Chapter 4

Is the Devil Inside
Directing Your Life?

To whom have you turned over the reigns to your life? Have you given the power to the devil inside[3] without realizing it? The devil inside is your inner critic. The devil inside is the part of you that thinks you are flawed, have problems, and are not a good person. The devil inside does not let you enjoy your successes and amplifies even the most minor of setbacks.

The devil inside thrives on low states of mind like fear, guilt, anger, resentment, and jealousy. The devil inside seduces you into believing that your every thought is fact, especially the negative ones. If you are not aware, you relinquish control of your life to your inner critic, and you don't realize that your inner critic is not you.

It's My Party

Imagine that you are at a crowded party. The din of conversation reverberates throughout the room. No matter where you situate yourself, the volume is overwhelming. A friend of yours attempts to speak to you from across the room but no matter how hard you strain to hear, you can't. Suddenly, someone drops a glass and it shatters. All conversation comes to a complete halt as everyone turns to see what happened. As your friend calls to you again, in the absence of party noise, you can hear her every word clearly and easily.

The constant noise from the party conversation is just like the mental chatter of your inner critic. The voice of your friend is your inner wisdom. **When your head is filled with the noise of your own thinking, you can't hear your own wisdom.** Cut off from this guidance, life will not work as smoothly. Your inner critic is particularly adept at drowning out your inner wisdom.

The good news is that your inner wisdom never leaves; it's just occasionally overwhelmed by the devil inside just like your friend's words at a party were drowned out by the partygoers.

To reconnect with your inner wisdom, all you need to do is stop listening to your inner critic. No matter how authoritarian your inner critic may sound, it is not the voice of Authority. If you ignore your inner critic long enough, it will grow tired of pleading on deaf ears.

Distinguishing Your Inner Wisdom

At the end of 1998, my wife and I were at a crossroads. We were madly in love and had enjoyed being married for over 9 years. Like any other couple, we occasionally had disagreements, yet we always were in sync on the things that mattered most. We enjoyed each other's company, and we knew deep inside that we were meant to be together.

We were now at an age when the decision to have children was omnipresent. We really struggled with it. Some days we thought we would love to have children, and others we were sure that we would not.

We finally settled in to the idea of just being a couple. Consequently, not wanting my wife to have to continue with birth control, I decided to schedule a vasectomy.

I made an appointment with a physician and scheduled the procedure. Everything was fine until the day before the appointment. And then something happened, something completely unexpected...my wisdom spoke to me.

It was not a voice I heard, it was more like a feeling. It was a deep and powerful knowing. I just knew that going through with the procedure would be a monumental mistake, and I was very clear that it wasn't simply fear of being cut in a very vulnerable place. It was one of the strongest knowings I'd ever felt.

Without any further debate and logical reasoning, I announced to Monica that I wanted to cancel the surgery, and I said to her, "Let's have a baby, instead!" With the proclamation came a tremendous sense of excitement and even a bit of fear that made me feel more alive than I had in a long, long time.

Inexplicably, Monica knew too. After months and years of "not knowing," in that moment we had peace and clarity. Within a few months, Monica was pregnant, and a little over a year from the day I heard my inner wisdom, we were blessed with a beautiful baby boy.

Thirteen years later, that young man has enriched our lives in ways that we never could have imagined. He has taught us valuable lessons. He has helped us see the world differently. And he has put us more in touch with our hearts than ever before.

How do you tell the difference between your inner wisdom and your inner critic? Everyone will experience their inner wisdom a bit differently. Some may hear a voice, some may have a feeling in their gut, others may have a strong sense of peace, and some may even see a vision.

Ultimately, your feelings let you know whether it is inner wisdom or inner critic. Your wisdom will be accompanied by a feeling of calm and peacefulness. You will feel completely at ease and on your game when you are receiving wisdom. On the other hand, your inner critic leaves you feeling out of sorts, anxious, and distinctly off your game. Do not let the words confuse you. You don't even have to identify it as wisdom. The label is not important; it's just a way to describe in words what is much easier to identify by your feelings.

Your feelings are your guide, and they always let you know the reliability of your current thinking.

Feelings of ease and well-being point to the reliable thinking of your deeper wisdom. Feelings of unease and confusion point to the unreliable thinking of your inner critic.

In my experience, there are a number of things that seem common for most people. Your inner wisdom is always kind, whereas your inner critic is rarely kind. Your inner critic is focused on the ego -- looking good, making a good impression, winning at all costs. Your inner wisdom has no interest in appearances; its only interest is your well-being and happiness. It will guide you to the most wonderful places, but only if you're able to hear it.

Just because you have an inner critic doesn't mean you should listen to her.

Your inner critic's language is filled with blame, excuses, rationalizations, and harsh assessments. Your inner wisdom doesn't deal in excuses and blame; it is only interested in gently guiding you in the best direction for you. If you want to hear inner wisdom, you must first learn to recognize the devil inside.

Then, you must be willing to ignore it, no matter how compelling its message. The inner critic is like the song of the siren; if you are not careful, it lures you in. Before you know it, you are under its spell.

Your inner wisdom, on the other hand, is often quieter and more subtle. The devil inside is anything but subtle. You will never have trouble hearing your inner critic; the challenge will be to ignore its persistent urgings.

Your inner wisdom is the key to your ultimate freedom. It wants the best for you. When you hear your inner wisdom, you'll know it. It's common to describe it with language like, "I just knew," or "it just feels right." Be patient, and be open to what it has to tell you.

Your inner wisdom belies logic and rational thinking. It may not always make sense or be what you want to hear, but it is **always** in your best interest.

Resist the need to rationalize or justify what your wisdom is prompting you to do. The reasons and logic will only confuse you. They will awaken your inner critic. Let your inner critic sleep. She's usually pretty busy; I'm sure she could use the rest. And if she's not tired, let her go shopping. You do know your inner critic wears Prada[4], right?

Coming Up ...

Have you ever wondered why sometimes you feel like you can conquer the world, and other times you're not sure if you can drag yourself out of bed? In the next chapter, you'll learn the amazing secret to why you feel the way you do, and the incredibly simple way to shift the tide back in the direction you want when you feel off your game.

Freedom Inquiry

How would your life be different if you were connected with your inner wisdom more often?

Chapter 5

Kick Off Your
Shoes and Relax!

Of all the chapters in this book, this one may be the most important. What if there is one critical, yet easily overlooked, factor that influences everything you experience? And what if you knew, not only exactly what it is, but how it really works?

There is such a factor, and you're about to gain an understanding that has the power to totally transform your life.

Examining Your Baggage

Imagine that you are a member of airport security personnel, and you are in charge of watching the monitor that shows the contents of people's carry-on luggage. Your job is to watch the computer monitor and interpret what you see on the screen as safe or dangerous, significant or not significant.

Item after item, bag after bag, shoe after shoe is sent down the conveyor belt through an X-ray machine that reveals the item to you on your monitor. If you simply observe and do nothing, the items pass down the conveyor belt, through the X-ray device, and out the other side.

If you decide that something you see is important, you may stop the belt and study the item carefully, consider it fully, and interpret its significance. If you need to run the belt backward and forward several times to make sure, so be it. Because it is critically important that you ensure every item that passes through is safe, you must take painstaking measures to be convinced you are doing the right thing.

In order to do your job efficiently, there is an optimal rate of speed of the belt that allows you to interpret things accurately without becoming overwhelmed or stressed. If the rate is too fast, accurate interpretation will be nearly impossible. The chaos will lead to errors-- errors which have major consequences. Your success as an airport screener depends on the reliability of the system and knowing how to use that system to maximize your performance.

The Thought-Feeling System

The airport screener system is much like the human thought-feeling system. Your ability to thrive as a human being also depends on understanding how to use that system to maximize your performance. Fortunately, this system is 100% reliable and never breaks down.

The thought-feeling system has two "devices" that work together to allow us to observe our own thoughts -- our brain and our consciousness. We have a conveyor belt of infinite new thought and fresh ideas. These thoughts flow to us on a regular basis.

When nothing is present on the conveyor belt, nothing appears on your monitor. When there is no thought appearing in your consciousness, there is no experience of life. If you are standing at the rim of the Grand Canyon, and you have no ability to think, you will have no experience of the Grand Canyon. It is thought that creates the experience.

There are two ways to cut off access to the innate wisdom provided by the "conveyor belt" of new thought. One is by pausing it to engage in a specific thought. If we hold onto the thought too long, we call this over-thinking. While this is useful to the airport screener, there are consequences to us doing that. Over-thinking blocks the flow of fresh thinking temporarily so nothing can get through.

The second way is by ramping up our own thinking. Much like speeding up the conveyor belt too much, when our mind is overly busy, we lack clarity and often make poor choices. **Fortunately, our thought-feeling system will automatically return to its natural speed once we stop engaging with every thought that we think.**

All you can ever experience is your own thinking.

Experiencing peace of mind, happiness, and well-being in any moment is a result of recognizing that every thought appearing on our monitors is not significant - unless we decide it is. If we let thoughts pass through unencumbered, they can have no effect on us. While it's easy to see that some thoughts are harmless, thoughts like "I wonder why cats sleep so much?" or "It looks like it might rain today," other thoughts can often have the appearance of being much more important.

Like the airport screener, you **decide** whether something is safe or dangerous, good or bad, important or irrelevant. **You are effectively making it up.** So what you **choose** to make up creates your experience.

The trouble occurs when you forget that you made it up, and begin to treat your thoughts as if they are real.

The good news is that when you wake up and realize you forgot you were making it up, you don't have to do anything. The conveyor belt of new thought has never stopped running.

So, is engaging with my thoughts a bad thing? Do I need to worry about the content of my thoughts? Fortunately, the answer is No. If the airport screener makes an error in judgment or gets distracted and misses a dangerous item, the consequences can be catastrophic.

You, on the other hand, don't need to be so vigilant. **You don't need to protect yourself from negative thoughts, and you don't need to replace them with better ones either.**

The worst that can ever happen to you is you forget that it's only your thoughts creating your experience. Once you recognize what's going on, there's nothing to do. After all, a new thought is always on its way.

You are free to live the life you want even when your thinking is not cooperating. You can engage with the thoughts you choose to and let others go. **Once you really see how the thought-feeling system works to create your experience, you are truly free.** Then, you can kick off your shoes and relax!

Coming Up ...

Have you tried unsuccessfully to change your behavior through willpower and self-discipline? Have you tried strategy after strategy based on the advice of experts? In the next chapter, you will learn a vastly superior pathway to fulfillment, stress-free living, and creativity.

Freedom Inquiry

How would your life be different if you spent more time observing and less time interpreting?

Chapter 6

Understanding is the New Black

Are you giving away your own power to experts?

How do you know when outside advice, a change in behavior, or adapting a new strategy makes sense for you?

Have you lost touch with your innate wisdom and guidance?

Without the endless mind chatter, would you be able to see the circumstances of your life more clearly?

When your mind is in a state of turmoil, it's easy to look outside of yourself for solutions. In fact, it can become your default strategy if you're not careful - asking other people, "What do you think I should do? What would you do?"

In those moments, the lack of clarity seems very real, and it compounds the notion that you don't have the answers.

Here's the dichotomy. When your mind's in turmoil, even the most sound and useful advice won't be easy to integrate. You're simply not in the frame of mind to utilize it. Not only that, it doesn't take into account who **you** are. How can it? It's from someone else's mind, perspective, and experience. At best, it's an educated guess.

When your head clears (trust me, it will), you won't need the advice anymore. You'll know exactly what to do.

But hold on a second, don't we need to learn skills and strategies sometimes? Let's take a look...

Oh, Behave!

If you want to be successful in any endeavor, doesn't it make sense to learn how to do it? Isn't following a "recipe" easier than making things up yourself? And doesn't that lead to more reliable results?

Certainly, there's some truth in that but I'd argue that we overvalue telling people what to do and not do. It's the de facto way to dispense advice in magazines, blog posts, and books -- give people a step-by-step formula. We see this all the time with headlines and titles like:

• 5 Steps to a Happier You

• 7 Best Practices for Managing Stress

• 9 Sure-fire Ways to Book More Clients

I'm not saying all the advice is bad or will never work. Not at all. Some of is quite good.

Here's what I am saying --

When both the person giving the advice and the person receiving the advice don't understand how the mind really works, the opportunity for frustration goes up dramatically, and the likelihood of achieving the result you want is relatively low.

When the person trying to follow the advice is in a low state of mind, their thinking will be in the way. If you're the advice-giver, you'll be flabbergasted as to why they can't just do what you did.

You'll try pushing them harder, fixing their thinking, or just saying things louder (oh, yeah, that'll work--think trying to get your teenager to fold laundry) -- all of which will make them perform worse.

If you're the one trying to follow the advice, you'll be wondering what's wrong with you, what you're doing wrong, and maybe even, what's wrong with the teacher or their advice.

All the thinking that's required to follow the advice gets in the way of following it well. All the thinking that gets stirred up when it's not working, takes you further and further from your A-game.

It's a common mistake. We're so tempted to assume that if we want to be successful, we should mimic the behavior of people who've already succeeded. Copy their habits. Develop their mindsets. Take the same actions they took.

Unfortunately, this often doesn't work.

When we fail to look at what's really behind the habits, mindsets, and actions of successful people, we miss our own unique opportunity for greatness.

Greatness is a result of a clear mind. And in order to have a clear mind most of the time, you need to understand how your mind actually works. Otherwise, you'll tend to do things that clutter it up instead.

That's why I say, understanding is the key to success. With understanding, you won't get in your own way nearly as much. You'll consistently tap into your deeper wisdom, so in any situation you'll know what strategy makes sense and how to apply it.

There are lots of tidbits of wisdom out there that can create confusion. Let's take a look at one of the more prevalent ones.

Go Fish

Everyone knows the saying, "Give a man a fish and you feed him for a day. Teach a man to fish and you feed him for a lifetime."

Certainly you offer a greater level of service to your son by teaching him how to look up a library book in the catalog system, and then how to find it on the library shelf than you would by getting the book yourself and bringing it to him. Similarly, you serve your daughter at a much higher level by teaching her how to perform long division rather than giving her the answer when she asks you, "What is 171 divided by 3?" From that point forward, your son can find any library book in any library entirely on his own, and your daughter can now compute even the most challenging division problems without assistance. No one would dispute the benefits of teaching someone how to be self-sufficient.

But is teaching someone what to do the best we can offer?

Teaching a man to fish, while certainly better than just giving him a fish, is limited in its scope in a number of significant ways.

First, it's only helpful to the man when he is in a place where he can actually fish. Clearly, his ability to catch fish does him little good in the desert or in the middle of the city.

Second, there may be times when even after using everything he's been taught, the fish simply do not bite. No matter what strategy or technique the man tries, he does not catch fish. This may have nothing to do with the man's fishing acumen; it may be due solely to external factors beyond his control.

Third, there may be times when he discovers that he doesn't know how to catch fish in every situation. For example, if the man learned fly fishing or deep-sea fishing, he may not be adept at catching fish on a lake, especially if the lake is frozen.

Finally, and perhaps most importantly, the things he learns to be a successful fisherman have little or no benefit to other aspects of his life, such as his business, his tennis game, his marriage, his confidence, or his ability to master his finances. The teachings of the fishing instructor are limited in their reach no matter how brilliant the instructor is.

Now, I'm not saying it's not valuable to learn how to fish. If you want to catch fish, it's really valuable. So is learning to bake a cake, serve a tennis ball, or sell your services.

But without understanding how your mind really works, those skills will elude you at times. You'll get lost in your head and wind up trying to fix your thinking. And you'll make matters worse. Sometimes, a lot worse. You won't see a simple adjustment that would put you back on track. It won't occur to you to try a different approach. You won't realize that temporarily stepping away might be the best course of action.

Fortunately, there's a much better alternative. But before I reveal what it is, consider this...

What You See is What You Get

Imagine that you are driving in your car, and one day you notice that you're not reading road signs as well as you could. You suddenly realize that everything is a bit blurry. You are not seeing as clearly as you'd like. You make an appointment with your optometrist to have your vision checked.

Here is what the optometrist does not do. She does not advise you on a specific prescription. You will never hear her say, "You know, my prescription works really well. I am able to see perfectly so I recommend that you get the same prescription. Let me write it out for you. After all, if it works for me, it will work for you." You see the absurdity of that scenario.

If she were to issue her prescription to everyone, here is what would happen. On a very, very rare occasion, her prescription will match her patient's, and he will see perfectly. Sometimes, the patient's vision will improve, but only slightly. In most cases, the patient's vision will get worse.

The bottom line is this: the optometrist cannot advise you on a prescription. Why? The reason her prescription works is because it is based entirely on her seeing. No matter how great her prescription is, it cannot have the same effect on her patient because her patient's seeing will always be different.

This is the problem with advice. No matter how great the advice is, it is always coming from the advice-giver's perspective.

What's Your Strategy?

What about a strategy-based approach? Would that be better than telling you exactly what to do? Maybe. Maybe not. Strategies are certainly useful at times. The real dilemma is that just like advice, strategies point in the wrong direction. They lead you to look outside of yourself for solutions.

Back to our optometrist friend. Let's say she offers strategies to help her patients. Perhaps she suggests that her patient squint in order to see better. Or alternatively, she indicates that her patient would see better by moving closer to whatever he's looking at. These strategies might be quite useful - sometimes. They might work well - sometimes. But there will be times when they will not work, or situations where employing them would not be possible or just plain dangerous -- like approaching that cute little black and white kitty to give her a pet when it's actually a skunk. When you make a mistake like that, it really stinks!

When the strategies do not work, the patient is left assuming that the problem must be with him, or how he is executing the strategy. Pretty soon, he has an even bigger problem than the one he started with.

Instead of not seeing as well as he would like, now he has a squinting problem or a problem with exactly how close to the subject he should get. He is one step removed from dealing with his original dilemma of not seeing well.

If he continues down this path, he will forever be dealing with problems that are irrelevant to making his vision better.

The New Black is Understanding

Fortunately, there is another approach. One that points directly back to you. It places the power right where it belongs - with the expert on you - **YOU**. This approach is exactly what the optometrist will most assuredly use. She will show you to see more clearly on your own.

How Much *More* Freedom Can You Stand?
Are You All Tapped Out?:
Why Techniques Rob You of Freedom

Are you practicing yoga, meditation, mindfulness, tapping, and other techniques to calm your mind and reduce stress? Do you find when you're regularly practicing these techniques you feel better, but when you're not, you don't?

There is little doubt that these techniques can be helpful to those who practice them but to get the most benefit, it helps to understand why they work when they work, and what's going on when it appears they don't. The bottom line is -- I want you to be equipped to choose the techniques that are fun for you, and let go of the ones that no longer seem necessary. To learn how to take charge of your own well-being, independent of any technique or practice you may or may not be using, read the bonus chapter, "Are You All Tapped Out?" in the Freedom Folio. You can download your complimentary copy at **http://freedomfirstliving.com/freedomfolio**.

One by one she will share a new way to see, and let you notice what you notice. Do you see better or worse? Adjusting your vision until, at last, what you see is crystal clear. And once she finds that perfect prescription, you'll know how to see anytime that you want. All you have to do is put on your glasses.

Understanding is what allows you to see the world as it really is. It's also what will transform your experience of life.

Here is the simple formula for living the life you really want:

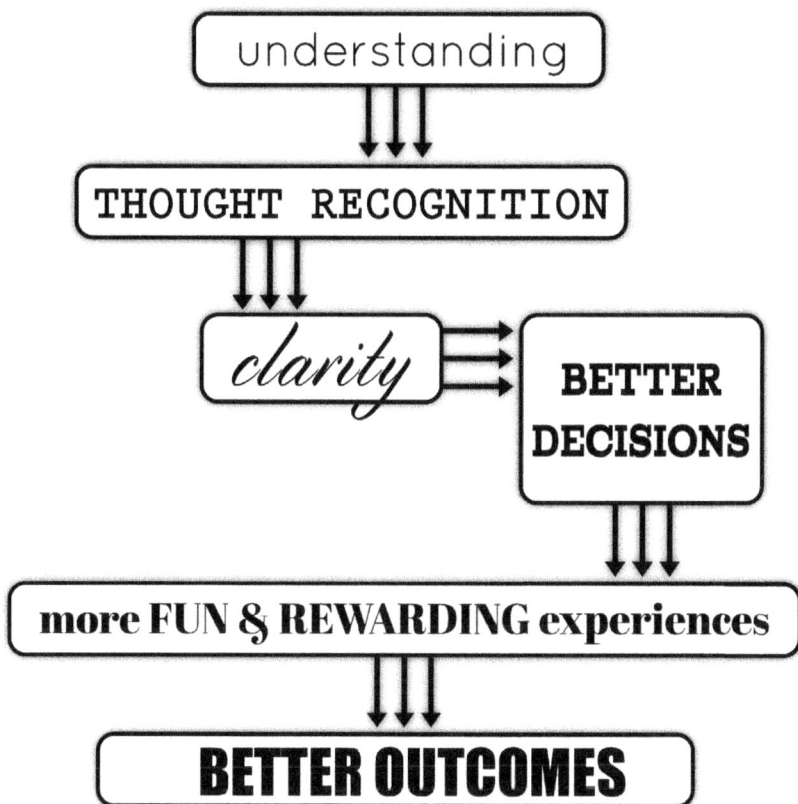

```
┌─────────────────────────┐
│      understanding      │
└─────────────────────────┘
            ↓↓↓
┌─────────────────────────┐
│  THOUGHT  RECOGNITION   │
└─────────────────────────┘
            ↓↓↓
┌──────────┐      ┌──────────┐
│ clarity  │ ⇒⇒⇒ │  BETTER  │
└──────────┘      │ DECISIONS│
                  └──────────┘
                       ↓↓↓
┌─────────────────────────────────┐
│ more FUN & REWARDING experiences│
└─────────────────────────────────┘
            ↓↓↓
┌─────────────────────────┐
│     BETTER OUTCOMES     │
└─────────────────────────┘
```

With understanding, you recognize thought as the only source of your emotions. With this recognition, you spend less time trying to fix things outside of you, so you spend more time with a clear head. You understand that the content of thought doesn't really matter -- it's just a reflection of your state of mind. Because thought is always changing, you know enough not to interfere. It'll

41

settle down on its own. So you wait out temporary states of muddled thinking and operate from clarity much more often. Which leads to much better decisions. From there, life is fun, fulfilling, and rewarding. In short, you thrive. You're more effective, creative, and productive.

Trying to intervene with better behavior and strategies ignores understanding. Teaching you to make better choices with no context for how and why to make them will only work some of the time. And when it's not working, you'll only make matters worse.

Even trying to elevate self-awareness is limited in value without understanding. If I'm more self-aware, maybe I notice I'm more effective when I get 8 hours of sleep and exercise regularly. I decide to commit to following those practices. When everything seems to be working, I relax and enjoy it.

But what happens when things aren't working the way you expect, even though you're doing "everything right?" Without understanding, you're bound to struggle.

Deepening understanding is always the most powerful place to make a difference.

With this foundation in place, better strategies and behavior will naturally arise out of your own wisdom, and you won't be fooled into turning them into universal strategies. Instead of seeing 8 hours of sleep and regular exercise as a panacea, you will see it as what makes sense for you right now.

Deeper understanding let's you take advantage of and apply new ideas more effectively.

Understanding leads you to add new skills and strategies from your own wisdom rather than fear-based thinking.

Understanding shines a light on thoughts of inadequacy, incompetence, and second-guessing, exposing them for the frauds that they are.

Understanding lets you pursue goals with a sense of ease and effortlessness.

When you understand the purpose your emotions serve, there's nothing you ever need to do to fix them.

Understanding shows you how to best use your time.

Understanding renders nagging doubts and worries meaningless.

Understanding keeps your mind free and clear so new, innovative ideas show up with regularity.

Understanding enables you to focus on the task at hand.

And it is repetition of the new skill or strategy, with as little interference and distraction from your thoughts as possible, that will produce the biggest gains. From there, it won't be long 'til you're back in black!

Coming Up ...

Wouldn't it be a shame if you were having a wonderful life and you just didn't realize it? Is it possible that happiness, peace of mind, and stress aren't out there somewhere, but much, much closer than you've ever considered?

In the next chapter, you'll get a glimpse at just how close you are to the life you're longing for.

Freedom Inquiry

What have you struggled to change about yourself that you know will change on its own with this new understanding?

Chapter 7

Welcome to the Freedom Hotel

As you go about living your life, it is incredibly useful to understand that you are always operating from a state of mind. This state of mind directly impacts the types of experiences you have and the quality of those experiences.

The Freedom Hotel

Once upon a time in a universe not unlike our own, there lived a troubled young woman. In the young woman's world, everyone resided in a shared dwelling, a place that came to be affectionately known as the Freedom Hotel.

For as long as the young woman could remember, she had lived in the appropriately-named Misery Wing. The Misery Wing was not a fun place to hang out. The furnishings were old and dreary. The smell of must and mildew pervaded everything. And no matter how hard she tried, she could never seem to relax.

The Misery Wing had many different floors, although they all looked essentially the same. The young woman had visited them all from time to time. They had names like Fear, Anger, Worry, Resentment, Guilt, Judgment, Jealousy, and Doubt.

One of the first things visitors noticed about the Misery Wing is that there were very few windows. The windows that did exist were extremely small, creating a dramatic sense of tunnel vision. The windows were so dirty that the view was quite unclear.

All of the furnishings and architectural elements in the Misery Wing, including the windows, sconces, and artwork, were all placed way down low on the walls. The extreme positioning of everything forced guests to always be looking downward; thus, magnifying the sense of hopelessness and despair that you felt. The entire design of the Misery Wing lent itself to pervasive pessimism.

The young woman thought it a bit strange that there were mirrors everywhere. She realized that she could not escape her own reflection unless she was looking out one of the minuscule windows. The abundance of reflective glass further reinforced the dramatic sense of self-absorption that was commonplace in the Misery Wing. Often, the young woman was so wrapped up in herself and her thinking that she bumped into the other people wandering around.

And boy, were there a lot of people! Despite the fact that it was not a fun place to hang out, the Misery Wing was almost always packed. There were people everywhere. Televisions blared the latest news headlines 24/7. The carpet was threadbare, the furniture was industrial, and the air was stale. Radios played nothing but divisive talk radio. And there was no way to change the TV or radio stations.

One day the troubled young woman discovered how easily she could move from floor-to-floor. Gradually-sloped ramps had been installed to make your rise or descent nearly impossible to distinguish. Of course, it mattered little which floor she was on. Her enjoyment of life remained more or less the same. As far as she was concerned, she was a victim of circumstance. She blamed the world, other guests, and the creator of the hotel for causing her to be stuck here.

She could not seem to stop her mind from swirling with chaotic thoughts. She couldn't remember the last time she had fun or even laughed. Whenever she did speak with someone else, which was getting rarer and rarer, she learned that everyone else felt the same way she did. They too were often paralyzed with fear and worry. Their stress levels ran extremely high. And, like the troubled young woman, their number one concern was self-preservation.

Her mind was so muddled that the young woman could no longer make decisions, at least not productive ones. She used to visit the Elevation Suite from time-to-time but she had long since given up on its promises. Whenever she passed it, she noticed people inside and wondered if it ever made a difference for them.

The Elevation Suite was an enormous room filled with every variety of treadmill, exercise bike, elliptical machine, and stair climber available. There was an area for lifting weights, a dance floor, and even karaoke machines.

In one corner was a stage featuring an unending stream of comedic performances. In another corner was a reading library stocked with uplifting, inspirational books and audio CDs. There were sofas spread throughout the room, and on the tables next to them were iPods® that you could pick up and listen to any time you like, as well as a wide variety of games that guests could play. In the center of the floor, there was a small meditation room that you could enter where sound-proof walls rendered every noise from outside inaudible. You could sit either on a comfortable mat or in a chair in complete silence.

There was a staff of therapists available to assist you. You were free to approach one and have an impromptu session if you so desired.

There was even an intricately designed glass door that led to a nature trail through a wooded garden with a small babbling brook that ran adjacent to the trail. Birds were singing, flowers were blooming, and the sun was always shining in the Freedom Garden.

The young woman had tried all that the Elevation Suite had to offer, and at times, she had experienced a glimmer of hope. Inevitably she would find herself back in the Misery Wing, and so eventually she saw no point in going back. Now every day felt like Monday to her.

One day as the young woman was wandering aimlessly, as she was now prone to do, she came upon a being so different from all the other guests that it took her by surprise. She stared in amazement at this older woman who looked so peaceful and full of joy. She almost continued on past but her curiosity got the better of her.

"Excuse me, Ma'am! I cannot help but notice that you look incredibly happy. Haven't you noticed what a miserable place this is?"

"Why this is the most exquisite place I have ever experienced in all my years," she replied. "I love living in the Tower of Freedom!"

Now the young woman had heard of the Tower of Freedom but she always doubted its existence. And one thing she knew for certain, this certainly wasn't it. In fact, she always thought the name, "Freedom Hotel," was a bit of a cruel joke. Perhaps this woman standing before her had gone so completely mad that she'd lost her mind.

"OK, tell me about this Tower of Freedom," the young woman insisted.

The old woman raved, "It's an extraordinary place. Everyone here is content and happy. There are many different floors, each adorned with the most beautiful artwork you've ever witnessed. Everything is placed high on the walls; there is nothing below eye level. There is an incredible sense of optimism amongst all its guests. Ornate tiles grace the floors and chandeliers adorn the ceilings. You will not find a single mirror in the Tower of Freedom. Guests here are not caught up in their own heads and consequently, form incredible connections with the other guests. People are able to see opportunity after opportunity in the Tower of Freedom. The floors have beautiful names like Joy, Happiness, Peace, Creativity, Enthusiasm, Humor, Passion, Inspiration, and Wonder.

The carpet in the Tower of Freedom is plush, and the wood flooring is immaculate. The fragrance of fresh flowers kisses the air, and the subtle sounds of classical music play gently in the background. The connections between the various floors are so subtle that you barely notice when they occur. It feels very spontaneous in that sense. Once guests get a taste of the Tower of Freedom, they never want to leave.

Life in the Tower of Freedom is simply magical. People report very little stress. They are not overly concerned with maintaining their personality. The velocity of thought is quite slow. Creativity is in abundance, and people produce results that amaze themselves and everyone around them. It feels like actions are effortless and guided by a higher power. It's easy to see the bigger picture. Laughter and fun are routine. Finding motivation or inspiration is never an *issue. Heck, everyday feels like Saturday. I am so grateful for the chance to live in this place!"*

The young woman was apoplectic. Surely this woman was delusional. Couldn't she see the utter despair that was surrounding her? And yet, she sounded rather sane. In truth, she sounded more sane than her fellow guests in the Misery Wing.

Finally, she had to ask, "Don't you see that you're in the Misery Wing? It's a horrible place! I know, I've lived here as long as I can remember."

"Ah, yes. The Misery Wing. I had almost forgotten about it. I once lived there you know. But you are clearly misguided. This is the Tower of Freedom." And she paused for what felt like an eternity to the young woman. "You see, one day I was wandering aimlessly through the Misery Wing much like you, and a thought occurred to me. A thought so radical, so different, so wonderfully magical that I couldn't stop smiling."

The young woman listened as her new acquaintance shared with her a story so unbelievably simple that she almost dismissed it. In an instant, the older woman had had an insight so clear that her life was forever changed.

She had suddenly realized that what she observed with her eyes, heard with her ears, and smelled with her nose was no more real than the thoughts she had about those things. In fact, what she had been feeling all day long was NOT the impact of her world but the impact of her own thinking. And it was those feelings that were influencing what she was seeing. From that day forward, everything changed. She has lived in the Tower of Freedom ever since, or so she says.

What the young woman heard amazed her, yet she couldn't seem to get past the fact that the older woman was stuck here in the Misery Wing. Perhaps this older woman was high from a trip to the Elevation Suite so she asked about it.

"Actually, I haven't been to the Elevation Suite recently, although I do visit from time to time. Now I go simply because it's fun and I want to go, not because I'm hoping it will get me somewhere. Turns out, there's nowhere to get to."

49

It occurred to the young woman that maybe she had it all backwards. Maybe what she was thinking was not a reflection of the reality of the world. Maybe what she observed about the world was influenced by her state of mind in the moment. Could that really be true?

She closed her eyes at the sheer magnitude of what she was beginning to realize and when they re-opened, they saw ornate tile, grand chandeliers, and stunning artwork. The young woman had miraculously made it to the Tower of Freedom!

She walked with the older woman happily enjoying this place that she had been sure didn't exist only moments before. And then without notice, a thought occurred to the young woman. "What if it doesn't last? I can't go back to the Misery Wing, I just can't. It's dreadful. I'd rather die than go back there." Sure enough, before she could think another thought, she was back in the Misery Wing again with the wise older woman still there beside her as happy as ever.

"What happened? Did I just imagine that?"

"Oh, no. It was real. And so is this. Here is the secret, my dear friend. If you will simply allow this beautiful system of yours to do what it is designed to do, you will live in the Tower of Freedom more and more often. And when you don't, although it will seem like you're in the Misery Wing, you'll quickly realize that it's only an illusion that will inevitably change if you don't interfere."

Epilogue

The Freedom Hotel comes with a great Rewards Program, and you are automatically enrolled and earn points just for living in the Tower of Freedom. The rewards are a wonderful life, joyful experiences, powerful results, incredible relationships, a stress-free mind, and a sense of freedom that makes life truly amazing! And the best news of all is even though you can check out from time to time, you can never truly leave[5].

*Chasing freedom is an unnecessary
mistake because you're already free.*

Coming Up ...

What if there were just one variable affecting your entire
experience of life, and you didn't know what it was? What if your
whole life could transform without having to change anything? It
can.

In the next chapter, you'll learn what causes you to feel the way
you do, and how you can use that information to transform your
experience regardless of what's going on.

Freedom Inquiry

When you are in a low mood or unproductive state of mind, what
occurs to you as the best approach to return to well-being?

Chapter 8

One Bad Apple[6]

Imagine you're in the produce section of your favorite supermarket. Everything looks fresh, bright, and vivid. Delicious mangos, succulent peaches, bright red tomatoes, luscious green grapes. Where do you start?

Your senses come alive. Right now, you're in the mood for a crisp, juicy apple. You wander over to a table teeming with apples. You're hungry so grab one and take a bite.

When you get that fresh snap and burst of flavor you love, you smile inside. You continue eating bite after bite, relishing the sensation of the crunching fruit on your palette until you've reduced it to its core.

If, on the other hand, the apple is soft and mealy inside, you're likely to gag. Maybe, you'll spit it out. Taking a second bite -- not gonna happen. Why would you keep eating a yucky apple? You wouldn't. That's just plain gross.

If you keep eating the bad apple expecting it to taste better, you'll be disappointed. Besides, you know that there are an endless supply of apples. If you don't like that one, you can pick a new one.

You don't have to eat mealy apples. You have taste buds that are there to serve you; they're the feedback mechanism that let us know if the apple is worth eating or not. If the feedback is positive, we keep eating; otherwise, we stop.

What could be simpler?

The same is true of the human experience. The challenge is seeing beyond the illusion to the truth about what we're "tasting." as we go about our daily lives. Despite how it appears, we don't experience people, circumstances, and events. We experience our thoughts about the people, circumstances, and events.

All we can ever experience is our own thinking. All we've ever experienced is our own thinking. All we will ever experience in the future is our own thinking.

Thought is the hidden variable that links people, circumstances, and events with our feelings, and that is what constitutes our entire experience of life.

It's never the first thought that creates a problem -- it's all the ones that follow.

Our feelings are the *taste buds* of the human experience. Stress, anger, overwhelm, jealousy, frustration, sadness, and other emotions we typically label as negative are our taste buds telling us we're eating a mealy apple. If we stop eating it, the bitter taste vanishes. You can't taste an apple you're not eating.

When you misinterpret the feedback your feelings provide and panic, you'll try to make the feelings better by changing the people, circumstances, and events. Lots of work, beyond your control, rarely succeeds. Tends to annoy others and often yourself. Totally unnecessary. That's like dipping the mealy apple in sugar to make it taste better.

Another panic response is to make yourself feel better by changing your thoughts. That's like polishing the mealy apple. It might look nicer but underneath it still tastes lousy.

It's not the content of your thinking that's the issue. It's that you belief your thinking reflects reality -- that your feelings are giving you information about the world. They are not. They're giving you information about the quality of your thinking and your state of mind.

You don't keep eating a mealy apple because you know you can just pick up a new, fresh one. Similarly, when you understand that thought is ever-changing, you won't waste your time indulging in the yucky ones. You know a fresh, new, juicy thought will come along eventually -- it always does. And when it does, you can savor it and enjoy its fruits.

When you're seeing clearly, your feelings let you know that your thoughts are trustworthy.

When you're not seeing clearly, your feelings let you know your thoughts are unreliable.

Pay the unreliable thoughts no mind, and they can't do any harm.

Pretty straightforward, isn't it? In fact, it's as easy as A-B-C[7]!

How Much *More* Freedom Can You Stand?

Too Stressed to De-stress:
The Simple Way to Be Free From Stress Forever

In a recent survey of 1000 people, nearly 60% reported being overly stressed in one way, shape, or form more than half the time. Whether feeling overwhelmed with too much to do and not enough time, trying to control outcomes, or judging themselves harshly for not doing better, the results point to the fact that without understanding, humans suffer. Are these results surprising to you?

To me, the ultimate irony was the six different ways to dissolve stress offered by the surveyor. Can they work? Sometimes. Are they helpful? Not really.

I want to help you simplify your life -- if you're like me, you don't need more things to do and practice. To read the bonus chapter, "Too Stressed to De-stress," and learn why such well-meaning advice may be creating more stress than it resolves, go to **http://freedomfirstliving.com/freedomfolio**.

Coming Up...

Do you ever struggle with your relationships wondering how you can build a closer connection with those you love? Would you like to have a more collaborative, team-focused rapport with your colleagues and co-workers?

In the next chapter, we'll find out the secret to what makes great relationships thrive.

Freedom Inquiry

What benefit do you see in no longer *"eating mealy apples once you notice they taste bad?"*

Chapter 9

Everybody's Right
and You're Always Wrong

If the title of this chapter has provoked anger in you, fear not. The title could just as easily be, "Everybody's Wrong and You're Always Right." I purposely made the title provocative to ensure that you would read it. I guess it worked!

This principle has the power to transform your relationships instantaneously once you really see the meaning behind the title. Your level of compassion for others will rise dramatically, and you'll ...

• More readily accept others for who they are.

• Find it far easier to be around people with whom you don't always see eye to eye.

• Experience far less stress when you don't always have to prove how right you are.

And you'll be happier and more peaceful in your relationships when you see that rightness and wrongness do not exist.

Everybody's Right

There are many variables that affect how we see the world in any particular moment. These variables include:

- Your current mindset and state of emotions - fear, anger, creativity, enthusiasm, etc.
- The operating frequency you are tuned to - problems are everywhere, opportunities abound, my spouse doesn't care about me, my spouse is a beautiful, loving person
- The thoughts that you are thinking
- Past experiences

Based on these variables, you will interpret events, circumstances, the behavior of other people, the state of the world, and your own abilities accordingly.

Let's say your spouse is stressed-out, tuned to look for problems everywhere, and has had some difficult experiences in the recent past.

When he gets a call from one of his clients canceling an important contract he was expecting to sign, he will likely interpret the call as a major crisis. He may lash out and complain to you that you don't do enough to contribute to the family finances and that you never have.

Your first thought might be that he's wrong, and you're right. You could very easily get defensive and blame him for not working harder to develop new business instead of relying on existing clients. Soon you could have a major disagreement on your hands, and a verbal fight could ensue. Except that you remember the title of this chapter and are reminded that he is right, and you are wrong.

Why he is right is because given all of the variables we mentioned above, his interpretation of a particular event or circumstance is highly predictable. In fact, if you could step into his body and suddenly experience exactly what he is thinking and his current state of mind, you would interpret the exact same circumstance the same way he did. Given what he is seeing, the conclusion that he draws is exactly right.

If any of the variables changes, he will draw a different conclusion. The more the variables change, the bigger the difference in the conclusion that he draws.

What is constant here is that no matter what conclusion he draws, it will be completely accurate based on the state of the variables. In that sense, he is right, and so is everybody else. Of course, it stands to reason that so are you.

You're Always Wrong

You might want to show this to your spouse (or teenage kids). They will get a kick out of it. After all, they've known all along that you were always wrong. To finally see it in print would really make their day.

At the end of the last section, I stated that you, too, are always right, so how can it be that you are always wrong?

Here's how ...

For every interpretation of an event, circumstance, other person, the state of the world, or yourself, you would reach a different conclusion if you were seeing things differently.

Therefore, whatever your interpretation is cannot be right if there are other interpretations you would reach if you were seeing the situation differently. In that sense, you are always wrong and so is everyone else.

The Restaurant[8]

Imagine that you are having a romantic anniversary dinner in your favorite 5-star restaurant with your partner. You are laughing and enjoying each other's company a great deal. As you are talking, you hear a sound behind you that sounds like a cough or maybe a sneeze, and then you feel a mist on the back of your neck. You decide to let it go; it's your anniversary after all.

Then it happens again, only this time it's a little bit more mist. Again, you decide to ignore it and focus on how great your partner looks tonight, and how great the food tastes. The third time you feel a large spray on your neck is the last straw. You turn around to really give this inconsiderate lout a piece of your mind when you see that the man is choking.

Instinctively, you jump out of your chair, run behind him, and perform the Heimlich Maneuver. Thankfully, you are able to dislodge the piece of meat that caused the obstruction and save the man's life.

When you had the thought that you were being coughed or sneezed on deliberately, your interpretation was that you were being disturbed by an inconsiderate lout. **As soon as you saw the situation differently, you reached a different conclusion**.

The original interpretation was clearly wrong; he was not an inconsiderate lout.

At the same time, the original interpretation was also right because it was the only conclusion that could be drawn given the thoughts and state of mind you were experiencing.

Whether someone has a bit of food lodged in their windpipe or a discouraging thought lodged in their consciousness, they will do whatever they know to do to get relief from the obstruction.

When you can see clearly the source of their outward distress, it requires no effort to show compassion.

Avoiding Relationship Regret

I have been married to my best friend and the love of my life for 24 years, and we've been together for more than a quarter century. Our relationship thrives and gets better with each passing year, and yet there have been moments over those years when we have disagreed about something. Someone did something unwise (yes, that would almost always be me), and it caused the other person to feel unloved.

In the heat of the moment, thinking can look mighty real. When my wife and I have a disagreement, it's often accompanied by some extreme thoughts. When I'm really angry, frustrated, or disappointed, I've had the thought that maybe I'd be happier being single. In those moments of clouded vision, I have had the thought that she'd really be sorry if she didn't have me around anymore. Let's face it, everyone who's ever been in any kind of serious relationship, romantic or otherwise, has had moments like these.

What saved me from taking impulsive action that I'd certainly regret is an instinctive awareness that these thoughts probably don't reflect how I actually feel. What I was feeling was temporary and tainted by a poor state of mind. I always told myself in these situations that if I still felt this strongly in a week, then maybe there was something to those thoughts.

What kept me from making things worse? As angry or hurt as I was, I knew that it wasn't my wife or her behavior causing my pain. It was the way I was seeing things that was causing me to feel that way. I didn't have to do anything but wait for the feelings to pass, and every single time what I discovered is, I'm madly in love with my wife and couldn't imagine my life without her. My thinking wasn't real at all.

It bears emphasizing this point - whether in relationships or any other area of life, thinking produced from a low state of mind is not reliable.

By allowing your thinking to shift on its own and waiting to draw conclusions about your relationship or make significant decisions until you are in a higher state of mind, you will always be acting from a place of clarity. What you see from that place, I assure you, will be dramatically different than what you see when your emotions have a hold on you.

Which is It? Right or Wrong

If you can be both right and wrong at the same time, which one is correct?

I assert that it is neither. There is no right or wrong. In order for someone's interpretation of a person, event, or set of circumstances to be right, that implies that there is only one way to see that person, event, or set of circumstances. As we have just seen, and already instinctively know, there are as many different interpretations as there are people on the planet.

Even the same individual will interpret the same event differently when they are in a different state of mind.

Everyone, including you, is absolutely doing the best they can in any moment based on the variables that affect how they see the world.

As one's state of mind changes so do one's perceptions.

When you can truly see that everyone, including you, is neither right nor wrong in a given situation, your life can truly transform.

The space in your thinking that is willing to consider another possibility than the one you are seeing, is the space that makes a change of heart possible. And it turns out that any relationship chasm, no matter how wide, has the potential to be healed with a simple change of heart.

The path to more loving, fulfilling relationships might be far simpler than you realize. If you are willing to do three things, your life and relationships can absolutely transform:

1) Recognize that the number of interpretations of any situation is infinite, depending on state of mind, current thinking, past experience.
2) Resist the temptation to judge.
3) When you do judge, and you will, be open to a change of heart.

As your conviction about right and wrong in any situation softens, the possibility for transformation exists. As I have seen first hand, there is a tremendous amount of freedom in not judging everyone as right or wrong...including, perhaps most of all, judging yourself.

Coming Up ...

If you knew that no matter how you see the world, you were only seeing a tiny fraction of the possibility that exists for you, do you think you would be open to seeing more than you currently do?

In the next chapter, we will take a compelling look at the way human beings limit themselves so that you can break free from those self-created prisons.

Freedom Inquiry

Reflect on the last argument you had with someone. How would that experience have changed if you could have seen where the other person was "right" and where you were "wrong?"

Chapter 10

Music to Your Ears

When you tune in to your local country radio station, you don't expect to hear Ozzy Osbourne singing, "Crazy Train." By the same token, when you are listening to the hard rock station, you probably won't hear "Cherish" by Madonna. Those things simply don't happen. Yet, what we often don't realize is that we're tuning into our own internal frequency every moment of every day.

We don't see the world as it is. We see the world from the frequency we're tuned into. And what we are tuned to see, hear, and look for has a monumental impact on our experience of life.

Given that, it would stand to reason that setting your dial to the best frequency for the outcome you want to create would be the most practical thing you can do.

At least, that's what I used to think. My early coach training and most of the prevailing logic today can be summarized as:

If it's going to be, it's up to me.

Power Through

If you want happiness and success, why leave that up to chance? You're a powerful being with the ability to choose. Why not tune to the frequency you want? You can control the stations you choose to tune to. Pick good ones.

That logic used to make sense to me when I thought that happiness and success were things to pursue. The truth is the empowerment approach worked for me occasionally but often failed miserably. Or more accurately, I failed miserably when I tried to do things that other people, especially experts, said were the right things to do, even though they didn't resonate for me.

That left me with one fairly substantial dilemma -- I thought the problem was me! I must be doing something wrong. I wasn't powerful enough or strong-willed enough. Maybe, heaven forbid, I just wasn't meant to be successful.

I tried everything to no avail. Until I saw something I had not seen before. Thanks to some wonderful mentors and teachers, I came to the realization that the frequencies we tune to are not mysterious, elusive, secret portals on a cosmic radio dial; they are our own, ever-changing states of mind.

The "Everything is a Problem" Station

When I was really struggling, I had innocently gotten stuck on the "Everything is a Problem" station, only I hadn't recognized how I got there and what could set me free. Perhaps you've had the experience of landing there yourself?

This is how life **occurred to me** from this frequency:

Neutral Event: *I'm driving to work, and there is traffic on the freeway.*
Interpretation: Problem.

Neutral Event: *I get to work, and the report I've been working on has disappeared from my hard drive.*
Interpretation: Problem.

Neutral Event: *The boss wants to see me to discuss my report ASAP.*
Interpretation: Problem.

Neutral Event: *My wife phones and says she'll be home late so I'll be in charge of dinner.*
Interpretation: Problem.

Neutral Event: *I catch a headline on CNN that the housing slump is likely to continue for several more years.*
Interpretation: Problem.

You get the idea. Neutral events (all events are neutral by the way) are interpreted as problems, not because they are, but because the frequency I was listening on was staticky.

Have you had that experience before? Things that sometimes roll easily off your back, at other times, feel like the final straw.

What causes you to struggle is not that you're noticing problems, it's that you don't recognize the reason why. Your ever-changing state of mind is the culprit. Unless you lock in the station, it will shift on its own. When it does...

The "I See Opportunity Everywhere" Station

The same neutral events take on new meaning. More productive options emerge. Your experience completely changes -- without doing anything to change it.

Neutral Event: *You are driving to work, and there is traffic on the freeway.*
Interpretation: Opportunity. Now you can listen to that podcast you downloaded to your iPod® before you get to work.

Neutral Event: *You get to work, and the report you've been working on is missing from your hard drive.*
Interpretation: Opportunity. Now is the chance to see if the new automatic backup/recovery system you put in place actually works, and a great time to include backing up your work to "the cloud" at the end of each day.

Neutral Event: *The boss wants to see you to discuss your latest report ASAP.*
Interpretation: Opportunity. Perfect! Now you can ask him about escalating your findings to the client.

Neutral Event: *Your husband phones and says he will be home late so you'll be in charge of feeding the kids dinner.*
Interpretation: Opportunity. Now you can take the kids to that fun, new restaurant you've been dying to try, but your husband thinks is too pretentious.

Neutral Event: *You catch a headline on CNN that the housing slump is likely to continue for several more years.*
Interpretation: Opportunity. Since you like where you live and plan to be there for awhile, it's probably a great time to refinance your mortgage since rates are at an all-time low.

So what's the relevance of this understanding? What difference does it make to your ultimate success?

Why It Matters

If you are a business owner, how often does an unproductive state of mind produce the following types of thoughts?

• I am a failure.
• The economy is challenging.
• Times are tough.
• I have to lower my fees.
• You cannot find quality employees these days.
• Clients are too demanding.
• Competition is fierce.

How does that leave you feeling about your prospects for long-term success or even surviving the week?

If you don't have an understanding of state of mind, it's very likely that the innocent thoughts above will create some very uncomfortable feelings. To free yourself from those feelings, you will look for a solution but you'll be looking through a serious fog.

You may end up making poor decisions such as:

- Lowering your fees
- Taking on difficult clients
- Agreeing to work that doesn't inspire you
- Firing a valuable employee
- Taking shortcuts in your work
- Going out of business

When you have the understanding to allow these **TEMPORARY** low states of mind to shift, suddenly the whole world looks different:

- Opportunity is everywhere.
- Despite the economic climate, I find creative ways to serve my clients.
- It may be time to increase my fees and add more value.
- I enjoy expanding my team with extremely committed, high performers.
- There are always fun, new ways to astonish my clients.
- My competitors keep me on my toes and push me to innovate.

Writer's Block

Here's another common scenario that my clients regularly face -- a motivation block. They can't seem to find their mojo anymore. They love their work, or at least, they think they do. For some reason, they can't summon the desire to take action.

Let's look at a common one that everyone can relate to -- writer's block.

Imagine you want to write but you're just not feeling motivated. The frequency you're tuned into at the moment is completely scrambled. You have a couple of options:

1) You could do something to shift your mood.

This may or may not work. If you're doing it from static-filled thinking, my guess is you'll struggle. When you have an intuitive spark about what you'd love to do instead, you'll thrive. Keep doing that and eventually motivation will return.

2) Or recognize that the static is a sign of a low mood which tells you that your thinking is unreliable at the moment.

Therefore, you ignore the notion that you're not motivated to write. So you sit down to write. Soon enough your thinking shifts, and your mood shifts too.

The key to happiness, peace of mind, and being your best is to have no preference for what you see. Let your instincts guide you. The lack of mental noise will allow you to respond quickly to the guidance that comes through.

Know this - if you decide not to write, whatever thoughts you have about yourself are also not trustworthy. The idea that I need to write or I'm supposed to is simply arbitrary.

Here's the big mistake that most people make -- concluding that the solution is to just write anyway, even when you don't feel like writing. In fact, there's a very popular book based on this entire premise. The author asserts that we are at war with this internal resistance, and every day we must go to battle to slay the beast within.

Prescribing specific behavior as a resolution to a circumstance is flawed. It ignores the most important variable in human behavior - state of mind. Sometimes, it will be your wisdom talking when you conclude not to write. Other times, it will just be your noisy mind.

To be fair to the author, more often than not, it's the noisy mind doing the talking. Just getting down to the business of writing makes perfect sense when that's what you really want to do but your cluttered mind is getting in the way.

When your state of mind is clear, you don't need to do anything. You will naturally choose the best stations.

When your state of mind is noisy, you won't be able to find a decent station no matter how hard you try.

People who push and will themselves to find the best station don't realize that their efforts actually take them out of the present moment by introducing more thinking to the system. It also promotes the illusion that you have control of the system.

When you stop dwelling on unproductive thoughts, you're left with a beautiful feeling called peace of mind.

Those who do succeed with this approach, many times do so at an unnecessary cost.

There can be value in "tuning in" to something specific when you really want or need to see something. The critical difference is the state of mind behind the decision to "tune in." When it's clarity and wisdom, trust it. When it's blindly applying a universal solution, slow down and let your state of mind clear before making any decisions.

For example, it took me more than 3 years from the time I started writing this book until it finally went to print. There were many times I could have given in to external pressure, staticky thinking, and blind commitment to goals to "just get the book out there already." Something inside me let me know it wasn't time yet -- that is, until it was. When it was, the signal was loud and clear.

Anyone?

We've all had the experience of tuning out a boring teacher. The one who drones on and on in a monotone voice like the history teacher in *Ferris Bueller's Day Off*. You don't have to try hard to ignore what he's saying. It's effortless.

What about when you're in a class where the teacher is spewing out fact after fact and you're trying desperately to take notes fast enough to keep up. Then, mercifully, one of your classmates has the nerve to ask, "Will this be on the test?" As soon as the teacher utters that, in fact, it won't, you immediately put your pen down and relax! Why, in both of these situations, do you effortlessly stop paying attention? Because you see clearly that it's no longer productive to listen.

It's no harder to stop paying attention to your own unproductive thoughts when your state of mind is low.

Because they're your own thoughts, they seem much more compelling. That's the dilemma. But the simple truth is this -- thoughts are only worthy of your attention when your state of mind is productive; otherwise, you can safely ignore them.

It's not hard to see that if your operating platform in life is to find problems, you'll find them.

Since we tend to see what we're looking for, it would seem to make sense to purposely tune in to what you want to see. In other words, change the station to one you like. That can work for a while but what happens when they play a song you don't like? Of course, you can change the station.

Here's the thing...

You can live your whole life with your hand on the dial, constantly looking for a good station. Look around -- you'll see most people living that way. It's a stressful way to be. Not only that, you'll miss countless opportunities.

There's a much better alternative...

Allow your thinking to function without interference, much like a radio's perpetual scan mode. Sometimes it will land on something you like. When it does, stop and enjoy listening. When it switches to something you don't like, stop listening.

Nothing could be simpler. When you recognize the true nature of thought -- it is as random as the songs that play on the radio -- you will experience it as background music gently playing in the corner. You will be free to enjoy the experience and notice opportunities when they present themselves.

When you stop listening to the useless noise in your mind, what you'll find is that it will land on things you like much more often. And when it doesn't, no big deal. It will shift again soon.

That will be music to your ears!

Coming Up ...

Have you been under the impression that you're viewing the world as it actually is? There are major implications to your happiness and success in making that mistake.

In the next chapter, you will learn how to avoid the unnecessary struggles that often result from failing to recognize that the world is not always the way you see it.

Freedom Inquiry

What would life be like if you didn't have the pressure of choosing the optimal frequency?

Chapter 11

What If Your Whole
Life Were a Lie?

Before you proceed to read the remainder of this chapter, it's important that you set down the book and complete the following exercise. Trust me on this; most people will tell them themselves that they'll circle back later to do the exercise. Don't let that be you! Take a few minutes now to gain valuable insights that most people never have.

Your Autobiography

DO NOT READ ON UNTIL YOU COMPLETE THIS EXERCISE.

Spend 15-30 minutes writing your autobiography beginning from your birth all the way up to the present day.[9] **You cannot get this exercise wrong so do not worry about the content or how much you write.**

Allow this to be a stream-of-consciousness exercise designed to capture your life's highlights. Write from the perspective of what you would love to share about your life with a new friend. When you have finished, you may continue reading this chapter.

Visit from an Angel

There was an old woman who lay in a hospital bed. She had lived a reasonably long life, and now her days were coming to an end. She had myriad illnesses, and she felt ready to exit this world. For many of her adult years, she had lived in misery. She complained that nothing seemed to go her way, and she judged everything in her life to be wrong.

One night, when all was quiet on her wing, an angel appeared over her bed. In a soft, barely discernible voice, the angel spoke to her. She asked the woman if she was ready for the next part of her journey. She replied, "Indeed I am. I have had enough of this life. Nothing I ever wanted came to pass. I worked at lousy jobs. Even though we travelled extensively, I didn't really enjoy it; my husband was such a bore. My son married a girl I just couldn't stand. I'm almost relieved it's over."

The angel responded, "Oh, my Dear. You must not say these things. For they are not true."

"What do you mean they are not true. They most certainly are. I experienced all of that and plenty more. If you have the time - well, of course you do - I could regale you with story after story of why my life was a complete mess."

The angel smiled knowingly. "I understand, my Precious. It saddens me that I have to do this with so many of your kind. Because you experienced something does not make it true. Let me show you something."

Amazingly, right before the woman's eyes appeared what looked like a movie screen. Across the screen appeared images of her loving her work, traveling the globe, laughing and enjoying romantic moments with her husband, and meeting her daughter-in-law for tea every week and relishing in their conversations. Her entire life looked completely different in the movie.

When the movie ended, the woman wiped tears from her cheeks and asked the angel what it was that she had just witnessed. The angel replied, "Why, that was the life you would have lived if you had not believed your every thought."

Liar, Liar

So what? Why do I need to care about this? Here is the bottom line. Much of what you believe about you, your life, and your world is a **lie**. Okay, I'm being a bit extreme here to make a point. It would be a bit more accurate to say that much of what you believe about you, your life, and your world is not absolute truth. They are opinions and interpretations based upon the unique individual that is you. Because each of us has different backgrounds, different experiences, different states of mind, and different genetics, we each form unique views of the world. That is why two people can observe or experience the same event and walk away describing it entirely differently.

I remember one of my son's Little League games where I was fervently cheering for our team (in blue). A player from the visiting team (in red), trying to steal home, slid into our catcher who blocked the plate and made a beautiful swipe tag. He was clearly out. How could the umpire possibly call him safe? Outrageous! He was clearly out!

Okay, that's my version of the story. Like many sports fans (and parents), I am adamant that I'm right; this is exactly what happened.

If you asked a fan from the visiting team, you might've heard a different story. The story might have gone like this, *"One of our boys made an aggressive play and stole home, sliding right under the catcher's late tag -- he was safe! What a steal! Great call by the umpire."*

Wait a minute. Two different stories, one event. How can both be right? They can't. Because neither is right. They're both right given the perspective and state of mind of the viewer, but that doesn't make them right.

The truth will likely come from the neutral observer who notes, *"A player in a red jersey broke from third base attempting to steal home. The blue team's catcher attempted to make a tag. The runner was called safe by the umpire. The majority of fans booed but some cheered."*

76

Question Your Thinking

Why are we so susceptible to overlooking the fact that the book we are writing about our lives is a work of fiction?

The time between what we observe and what we feel is virtually instantaneous. It looks like what we're experiencing is happening to us. We don't notice that there is a third component involved -- thought.

Your thinking isn't a reflection of reality, it's a reflection of your state of mind.

Coupled with the fact that the voice inside our heads sounds authoritarian and serious, it's not surprising that we believe everything it says. Why would we stop to question whose voice it is that we're actually hearing? **After all, we're not taught to question our thoughts.**

But it's in the questioning that true insights are revealed. The insights that lead to new ways of seeing allow us to transcend our circumstances. The brilliant teacher, Byron Katie, shares that all our suffering comes from believing our unquestioned thoughts. In the questioning, you will often come to see that your initial belief is, in fact, not true, or at the very least, there is another possibility that is just as true or truer.

Attachment

Have you ever worked on a crossword puzzle and stared at a clue for the longest time with no idea what the right answer could be? Have you wondered if the crossword writer has lost all his senses?

I was working a puzzle recently where one of the clues was: Rug. I racked my brain searching for a type of floor covering that would fit based on the letters I had. I attached to one way of interpreting the clue, and that was all I could see. That attachment blinded me to other possibilities. Because my seeing was restricted, the answer eluded me. When my wife came along and immediately saw the clue as a hairpiece, she had the answer: Toupee.

The only way to experience a breakthrough was to recognize that perhaps there was another way to see the clue that I had not considered. In this detachment, the space for a new possibility emerges, and suddenly, the answer comes to you beautifully and gently like a balloon drifting down from the heavens.

We tend to suffer the same kind of attachment blindness in our own lives. We quickly draw conclusions about the events, circumstances, and people in our lives, and the story gets written. Soon we attach to the rightness of this story, and now we are stuck with it. If it is a happy, wonderful story, things might be just fine. But all too often the story causes us pain. It leads to fear, worry, anger, guilt, jealousy, resentment, and other troubling emotions. All this suffering turns out to be based on an attachment to one of many possibilities.

Here are some examples of beliefs that people attach to that limit their possibilities for happiness, freedom, and success:

- The best way to market one's services is via cold calling, and I hate cold calling.
- The only way to win in the corporate world is to know the right people.
- My husband spends too much time at work and not enough with me.

- My children do not appreciate how hard I work for them.
- If I had studied a different major in college, my life would have turned out much better.

Just like with the crossword puzzle, if you can recognize that you are looking at only one possibility and are willing to open up to the many others that exist, your wisdom will provide you with the answer. And when you hear it, you will know.

Who Do You Believe?

Your mind has made it up - that is the nature of a belief. It is something you make up to make sense of your world. You don't just *believe* that you have brown eyes, or that you live in your town. These are facts most everyone would agree on.

Beliefs are something else entirely. Some beliefs are more grounded than others; that is, you might be able to get closer to consensus. With other beliefs, you might find it difficult to get anyone to agree with you. **Regardless of whether anyone agrees or not, a belief is just one of an infinite number of possible descriptions that one could attribute to a circumstance.**

Once you can see that the story you have made up is just one possibility, you can see that you're always free to rewrite it.

It's worth noticing that every single opinion can be proceeded with "I believe."

Let's look at some examples:

- I am a terrible writer. (*I believe that I am a terrible writer.*)

- I procrastinate too much on things that are really important to me. (*I believe that I procrastinate too much on things that are really important to me.*)

- I'm really depressed. (*I believe that I'm really depressed.*)

- My boss doesn't see the big picture. (*I believe that my boss doesn't see the big picture.*)

- My spouse doesn't really care about my feelings. (*I believe that my spouse doesn't really care about my feelings.*)

When you add the words, "I believe," in front of these statements, it becomes much easier to see that they are not facts. **Beliefs by their very nature cannot be absolute truths. If you have to believe something, then it is not a rock-solid fact.**

What if you replace "I believe" with "I have the thought?"

- I have the thought that I am a terrible writer.

- I have the thought that I procrastinate too much on things that are really important to me.

- I have the thought that I'm really depressed.

- I have the thought that my boss doesn't see the big picture.

- I have the thought that my spouse doesn't really care about my feelings.

Notice how that statement is more accurate and points to where your freedom lies -- **not making the thought meaningful.**

If you can recognize this within yourself and maintain that awareness, you will move quantum leaps forward toward a life of freedom.

Our stories about our life, our experiences, and our circumstances create invisible traps as tight and rigid as any real ones. The secret to breaking free is to recognize the illusion - whatever prison you're in is a prison of your own device. Since you created it, you can unlock the door and set yourself free.

If I Can See (Think) It, It Must Be Real, Right?

The human mind is an interesting machine. We process a mind-boggling amount of information every second. In order to make sense of our world, the mind must generalize, distort, and delete information in a profound way.

In the world of neurolinguistic programming (NLP), there is a saying that "the map is not the territory." To represent the earth, a 3-dimensional world, on a 2-dimensional drawing, in a scale that we can hold in our hands or at least view on a wall, information is discarded, generalized, and reduced in a massive fashion.

The same is true of our minds. Each of us makes our own unique representations of what we see, hear, touch, feel, taste, and think. Those representations are shaped by a variety of variables including: our mood (state of mind), previous experiences, and social conditioning. To make the mistake of thinking that our representations (the stories we create) are real is a profound one. It can, and often does, lead to stress, fear, worry, anger, frustration, bitterness, fractured relationships, addictions, bad habits, and poor performance among other miseries.

Where we get into trouble is that we have been taught virtually from birth that if we experience something, then it is real. If it weren't real, we wouldn't be experiencing it. But there is a subtle distinction that we are not taught.

What you are experiencing is not reality, it is your own thinking.

Whatever is going on inside of you (your state of mind) not only influences your thinking but how you interpret your thinking. **Consequently, although it absolutely feels like reality, it is but one possible version of reality - YOURS.**

It is your truth. It is a creation, a story. I am not suggesting that you are a fraud. Up until now, all of this mental story-writing has been happening without your awareness. Believe me, I know it feels real. I lived most of my life under the illusion that whatever I thought and felt was reality, and often, this confusion caused me tremendous mental anguish.

Once you become aware that your life, for better or worse, is the summation of all the stories you have made up to explain your experiences, you are FREE.

Without this awareness, it is like walking through life with a blindfold on. The lack of awareness causes you to periodically bump into things and hurt yourself. Once the blindfold comes off, you can see clearly, and you no longer bump into things (at least very rarely).

This blindness is the number one thing that holds people back and prevents them from reaching higher levels of success and happiness. It is like a horse fitted with blinders so he cannot see anything happening around him. He is forced to focus on one thing, the path in front of him, but he is blind to everything else.

Many successful people are similarly blind. They have reached their success based on something that has worked really well for them, for instance a specific marketing strategy or business system. If you are not careful, you can become so attached to one way of doing things, that you are unable to see differently.

Absolute Paradise

Your thoughts are largely random. It's your state of mind that influences what you see and how you interpret what you see. Seeing past the apparent reality of your thinking is the essence of freedom.

We have a great 3-day event here in Charlottesville every June called the Festival of the Photograph. This year's marquee speaker was Tim Laman, a brilliantly entertaining wildlife photographer who spent more than 8 years trekking in remote regions of New Guinea and parts of Australia to be the first person to photograph all 39 species of bird of paradise.

He wowed the audience with both still and video footage of his excursions. The one that really got my attention was the story of the Wahnes's parotia. The male of this amazing species goes to incredible lengths to woo a female. He finds the perfect spot on the forest floor, one with an open area and a perch spanning across it just slightly above. He meticulously cleans out every stray leaf and any other debris he finds. He then begins one of the most amazing and bizarre courting rituals you'll ever see.

From ground level, where Laman originally positioned his cameras, what you'd witness is both fascinating and humorous, but not all that spectacular. This smallish black bird folds his wings in a makeshift ballerina-like tutu and dances all across his pristine stage while a bevy of female onlookers assess his performance from the perch above. You might wonder why on earth these females would find this so compelling.

But Laman's open, inquisitive mind led him to a brilliant insight. He realized that it would likely be more interesting to observe this ritual from the female's perspective. When he mounted a third, remote-controlled camera above the perch aimed at the clearing where the male struts his stuff, he was blown away by what he saw.

"It's incredible how different it looks from above. You just see a black oval instead of a ballerina with a tutu on. The iridescence of the breast shield is so much brighter because it's catching the light from above. We also saw a bright patch on the back of the head we didn't know was part of the mating display. That was a real wow moment."

And so it is for each of us. We often get so attached to a perspective that we cannot see the real miracle that's available to us. Knowing that it's our current thinking that's limiting us makes it much easier to allow the space for miracles.

Thoughts are bland. Your state of mind in the moment provides the flavor - sour or sweet, bitter or zesty.

And it's the ability to see things differently (which is what your wisdom offers) that opens up the possibility for massive growth. Your strengths can often be your greatest weakness because your belief in them is so strong that you cannot see beyond them to new possibilities.

Real freedom comes from recognizing the difference between *your* truth and *the* truth. *Your* truth is the interpretation you have chosen to believe. In other words, it is what appears to be true from the state of mind you are looking through. *The* truth is what is true regardless of your state of mind. Here are some examples:

Your Truth:
I shouldn't have to work weekends.

The Truth:
Right now, my boss wants me to work weekends.

Your Truth:
My teenage daughter looks and acts so different. Next she'll be on drugs and drop out of school. Oh my gosh, she probably won't even go to college.

The Truth:
My teenage daughter dresses and talks differently than when she was younger. She's not all that different than me when I was a teenager. She's hasn't missed a day of school this year, and she's carrying a B average.

Your Truth:
I'm a failure at sales. I can't seem to sell houses like I used to.

The Truth:
I have sold two houses this quarter and listed three others.

When you attach to *your* truth as though it is *the* truth, you are severely limiting yourself. But only 100% of the time.

The real insight to get is … **if you can see that what you believe is but one of many possibilities, you allow the space for new thinking to emerge.**

On the other hand, if you believe that what you are experiencing is reality, change is far more difficult.

Okay, so your whole life may not be a lie, but it *is* unquestionably made up by you. In every moment, you get to choose what you believe, how you see, and what you conclude. And in those choices, your life is made. Honest. Would I lie to you, honey?

Coming Up ...

Have you ever felt really, really stuck trying to resolve a seemingly unsolvable problem? In the next chapter, we'll look at where the feeling of stuckness comes from and how you can always set yourself free.

Freedom Inquiry

Write your autobiography a second time, but this time, include only facts - no opinions, no assessments, no interpretation, no story. When you are finished, compare the two versions, and notice the differences. How does carrying around your story affect your happiness? Your mindset? Your results?

Chapter 12

Are You as Stuck as You Think You Are?

In the not too distant past, there was a woman who was very creative, talented, and full of potential, but somehow life had gotten in the way. She felt a bit lost inside and somewhat confused. One day she was out walking in the woods, as she often did when she wanted to spend time with her thoughts. On this particular day, she was unusually troubled about the lack of direction in her life. As she crossed under a large pine tree, she felt her foot disappear beneath the leaf cover. She stepped into a hole and felt something grab around her ankle. In a moment of panic, she realized that she was trapped!

At first, she didn't worry too much. Friends and family would surely come to rescue her. But as the hours began to pass, she had the horrifying thought that maybe she wouldn't be rescued. Fortunately, she had her backpack with her. As usual, she had packed a lunch and a couple of water bottles for the hike. Now she began to wonder how long she could make do with the provisions she had. She reasoned that she'd be okay for a few days, and she'd surely be rescued by then.

As day turned to night, a sense of hopelessness came over her like none she had ever experienced. It started with the simple thought that maybe no one would come in time. Then, she began to wonder if anyone even cared that she was missing. "Would anyone really notice?," she pondered. As she thought these thoughts, she began to feel more trapped. Sadness and anger filled her mind.

At some point, she must have dozed off, for as she awoke, daylight had returned to the forest. Her mind picked up where it left off the night before.

She began to think about how much of her life she had wasted doing things she didn't really want to do. She thought about how many opportunities she'd let pass. She thought about the loved ones she'd never shared her true feelings with. A deep sadness came over her, and she began to sob uncontrollably. At that exact moment, a hot air balloon filled with passengers, who would have surely heard her had she screamed for help, passed overhead but she never noticed it.

When her crying subsided, she began to worry about running out of food and water. Then a thought came that chilled her to the bone. What if a snake, a bear, or worse yet, a mountain lion wandered into this part of the woods? "I would be an easy mark, unable to move on my own," she thought.

As the sun set and night approached, when she had all but given up hope, a large owl alighted on a branch just above her. She was fascinated by the owl since the only avian creatures she had seen had been small songbirds. Suddenly, the forest silence was broken by a gentle, loving voice. It was the owl speaking to her.

The owl asked her what she was doing alone in the woods. "I'm caught in a trap, can't you see?" The owl nodded.

After a minute or two of silence, the owl asked, "What is it like to be caught in a trap?"

After a moment of reflection, she admitted that at first it was no big deal. She thought she would figure out how to get free, or at least, someone would come along to rescue her. Then, she began to sense the hopelessness of the situation, and deep sadness, anger, and resentment came over her. Now she was just depressed at the thought of being stuck.

After another minute or two of silence, the owl asked her a question she had not yet considered. "What would you do if you weren't caught in a trap anymore?"

She waited for what seemed like a long time before speaking. Then she told the owl that she would only do work that she loved. She'd be kinder and more understanding with her husband and loved ones. She'd breathe deeper and notice more beauty in the world. She'd write, paint, and dance; things she used to do but stopped because life got too busy. "I'd stop putting off the things that really matter to me, that's what I'd do."

With that, the owl made an announcement. "My dear, it is true. No one is coming to rescue you. Fortunately, you don't need them to. You have everything you need already inside you. Oh, and by the way, look down -- you're not really trapped. You just think you are."

At that the owl flew away. The woman lifted her leg out of the hole, and to her surprise, the wise bird was right. She was free, and as she caught one last glimpse of the owl in the distance...

She bolted awake. Shaking off the cobwebs of her deep sleep, she realized it was only a dream. Here she was safe and snug in her bed. Relief washed over her. As her head was just about to hit the pillow to return to a hopefully more peaceful sleep, she bolted upright again, partly in joy and partly in disbelief. She had a sudden epiphany -- Oh, my gosh! All the times I've felt stuck in my life, all I ever needed to do was wake up from the dream! Then she lied back down and slept better than she had in years.

On Stuckness

Isn't it funny that this is exactly what we so often do? We create a trap in our own mind so tight and rigid that we cannot see our way out. It paralyzes us, has us miss countless opportunities, and causes feelings of tremendous stress. **The thing is - it's never the external circumstances that create the trap we imagine, it is our thinking.**

Be clear, it's not your fault. We are not taught to question our thoughts, to explore their validity and discover for ourselves whether they are true. The voice in our head sounds like the voice of authority, so we accept everything it says as the truth and act accordingly.

Your freedom begins with this realization - wherever you feel trapped or stuck, know that it is your thoughts that have led you there. **You are only ever one thought away from freedom.**

Stuckness is a feeling that you experience when you've been thinking thoughts of limitation. When your thinking gets too narrow or circular, you will feel trapped.

It's like being lost and noticing that in your attempt to find your way, you keep ending up at the same fork in the road. This frequently happens when you attempt to "think your way through" a problem that seems real from an unproductive state of mind, but wouldn't seem like a problem at all when your state of mind improves.

> *The idea that we can ever experience our circumstances is one of life's grandest illusions.*

More thinking is not the solution. Step back. Create some space and stop thinking about "*the problem.*" You can do things to facilitate the shift in mindset, or you can go about your life and wait for the natural shift to occur. When you stop adding more thinking, you will begin to see things differently.

Once you see that the trap is not real, it's a creation of your mind, then you are free to walk away and create the magical life that is your birthright.

Whenever it seems that you are trapped, find a quiet place and give yourself plenty of time. Consult your higher self, your inner owl if you will, and wisdom and inner guidance will reveal itself to you in unmistakable ways.

Coming Up ...

Do you sometimes feel like your mind will just never be quiet? In the next chapter, you will find out how understanding one key aspect of the human experience can reliably lead you to a quieter mind.

Freedom Inquiry

What would be different if you no longer treated the thoughts about what is keeping you stuck so seriously?

Chapter 13

Is Your Thinking
Carbonated?

Imagine you are holding a bottle of soda, shaking it wildly as if you're trying to erase an Etch-a-Sketch. Go nuts on it! Within a few seconds, you should see tremendous bubbling action begin! You can almost feel the chaotic energy as you hold the bottle. Ready? 1-2-3 twist the lid open! I dare you! Go on. As the lid opens, the carbonated liquid spews forth like a spectacular volcano. You have a real carbonated mess on your hands. All over the floor, all over your clothes. Why in the world would you want to open the lid when you can see all that bubbling action, and you know it's going to explode? Great question. Back to that in a moment.

Now imagine you have a second bottle of soda that you shake equally vigorously. Don't hold back in the slightest. When you've gotten it all riled up, set it down and walk away. Leave it alone for an hour or two. Now imagine that it's a couple of hours later. You return and notice right away that all the bubbling action has subsided. As you pick up the bottle, the chaotic energy that was there before has disappeared. Now twist open the lid. Nothing happens, of course. The chaos that existed two hours before has been replaced by calm. There is no resultant mess; there is only peace.

The Mind is Like A Soda Bottle

The mind may be still, and then suddenly a thought pops in. Perhaps it's a mildly worrisome or stressful thought. We notice it and ponder it. We think on it some more -- in other words, we begin to shake the bottle. The more we add to the stressful thoughts, the more chaotic our mind becomes, just like the bottle. Soon, our mind is racing, our heart rate has risen, and we have a sense of doubt and fear about whatever it is we are contemplating.

Within a matter of moments, our minds become like the soda bottle, ready to spew forth at any moment. By expending lots of energy trying to figure things out, trying to resolve the past or control the future, we unknowingly shake up the bottle in a most vigorous fashion.

Then the real trouble begins. We twist open the lid. In other words, we make decisions from this place of chaos - we attempt to resolve conflicts with a loved one, we try to brainstorm ideas for a new business, or we attempt to figure out our life purpose. We take actions when our mind is racing.

When you don't stir it up, your thinking will naturally calm on its own.

And guess what happens. We make a big mess. The decisions we make, the conclusions we draw, and the actions we take from this state of mind often don't lead to the results we want. Sometimes they lead to exactly the opposite of what we want. So we churn up the bottle some more in an attempt to settle things down. But it doesn't work. And this cycle repeats itself day after day if we fail to recognize that WE are the cause of the mess.

We are the ones who shook the bottle. What we experience on the inside - our thoughts, our moods, our mindset - determines our experience in the world. The mess happens in the outer world when we allow ourselves to shake up our inner world.

What happens outside of us is a neutral event.

The state of the liquid in our soda bottle when we open the lid determines how we interpret the event - either a big mess or total peace.

That is how our life works; and we mistakenly think it happened *to* us instead of being caused *by* us.

A Natural State of Peace

When we choose not to make decisions, take actions, or try to think our way out of a thought spin, just like walking away from the soda bottle, things will naturally settle and calm with no effort required. We do not need to intervene, but we must be aware of what is going on inside the bottle.

Once we recognize the stillness in the bottle, we are able to open the lid, and the result is nothing but peace. Similarly, once our mind settles and the churning of thoughts has passed, so often an insight or a nugget of wisdom bubbles up - kind of like a lone carbonation bubble slowly rising to the surface. We could not see it with all the chaos and shaking. But now, in the peace and calm, wisdom guides us to the decision or action that we know without question is what we are meant to do.

Most of us spend unnecessary time trying to operate productively in a vigorously-shaken state. It doesn't mean we are bad or defective - **it simply means we have forgotten how the mind works.**

With the soda bottle, when we recognize it has been shaken too much, we know exactly what to do. And as you gain the same awareness with your thinking, you will also know precisely how to respond.

Allow your soda bottle (your mind) to settle and calm on its own without intervention. When it does, from that place, your decisions and your actions will take you to some amazing places.

How Much *More* Freedom Can You Stand?
On Second Thought:
Make Great Decisions Every Time

Have you ever felt like you've made a great decision only to find yourself questioning it minutes, hours, or days later? This is a common dilemma almost all of my clients bring up at some point. When you understand what's really going on, you'll discover with great relief that you're not your own worst enemy.

My desire is for you to consistently make quality decisions that lead to a life of ease, joy, and great results. To assist you to avoid falling victim to second-guessing and self-doubt, I've included a bonus chapter you can read in the Freedom Folio called, "On Second Thought." You can download your complimentary copy at **http://freedomfirstliving.com/freedomfolio**.

Coming Up...

If you're thinking to yourself that life would be great if you could just think positively more often, think again. In the next chapter, we will see why positive thinking is a poor long-term solution and why, thankfully, you can thrive without it.

Freedom Inquiry

For today, simply become aware of when your thoughts are stirred up (like the soda in the shaken bottle), and with the best of your ability, let them settle on their own.

At the end of the day, answer the following question: How did your experience differ by ignoring your chaotic thinking rather than acting or making decisions based on it?

Chapter 14

Positive Thinking
Positively Doesn't Work

As you begin to see the powerful impact your thoughts have on your experience of life and the results you're able to produce, you may conclude that the best way to insure your happiness and success is to control your thinking. If only you could think nothing but positive thoughts, life would be simply wonderful - so the thinking goes.

If you wander into the self-help section of your local bookstore, you are bound to notice dozens of books that espouse the positive thinking approach. And if you could sustain this positive-thinking lifestyle, then you would almost certainly live a wonderful life filled with freedom, happiness, and peace. So, if you're a positive thinker, and life is working for you, "Congratulations!" You don't need to change your strategy just because *I* say it doesn't work. But, if you're ready for an approach that far surpasses positive thinking in its effectiveness and sustainability...then read on.

The Path Away From Negativity

When I discovered the impact of negative, low-level thinking on my happiness and my results, I immediately was drawn to the positive thinking school. I worked with it for nearly a decade, and my overall experience of life definitely improved. After all, positive thinking certainly seemed better than the alternative. And yet, I was still subject to more ups and downs than I cared for.

At the time, I didn't recognize the limitations of positive thinking, I simply thought I wasn't good enough at it. If I could only meditate more and achieve a higher level of enlightenment, I would be able to think positive all the time. In the past several years, I have discovered a fundamentally better approach, and I finally saw the limitations of the positive thinking model. To my delight and relief, the issue wasn't a fatal flaw in me.

A Pessimist, An Optimist, and a Realist

Three people have planned a picnic outing with their partners on a glorious summer afternoon when a storm begins brewing in the distance. The pessimist notices the storm in the distance and declares, "Every single time we get some time alone together something bad happens. Maybe it's an omen." Pretty soon, a fight with her partner ensues, and indeed, the picnic is ruined, even if the storm never comes.

The positive thinker notices the storm in the distance and thinks, "Our picnic might be ruined. It's going to rain." Then, she quickly realizes her error and corrects the thought, "It's not going to rain. Today is going to be a perfectly sunny day." When the storm comes, the positive thinker is disappointed and assumes she did not think positively enough or in some way made a mistake. If the storm doesn't come, the positive thinker takes full credit for the power of her thinking. Which only leads to a bigger fall the next time the positive thoughts don't lead to the result she wants. Either way, the positive thinker will eventually be confronted with the reality that she cannot control her thoughts (or the weather!).

The realist notices the storm in the distance and briefly thinks, "Our picnic might be ruined." Then she decides to enjoy the picnic while the sun is out, and recognizes that the storm may come or it may not. So the realist stays in the present moment and enjoys the day no matter what happens.

Why Positive Thinking Doesn't Work

There are three reasons that positive thinking positively doesn't work. **First, it lures you into the notion that there is a right way to think.** And if there is a right way, and you notice that you're not doing it, you're hamstrung. You won't be able to get anything useful accomplished. Your results will suffer. Your life won't turn out the way that you want. If you don't get this right, you are doomed. This sort of defeats the purpose of positive thinking-- don't you think?

The second reason positive thinking doesn't work is that, if deep down, you actually believe the negative thought more than the positive one, nothing will change. If you have the thought "I am a failure" and try to replace it with "I am a success" but you don't believe you are a success, the positive thought will not work, which is why many people who work with affirmations get frustrated or give up. They don't really believe the positive statement.

The third reason positive thinking doesn't work is that it is not a realistic strategy -- no matter how hard you try, you cannot control the content of your thoughts. You have no control over the thoughts that enter your consciousness. Certainly not over an extended period of time.

Positive thinking is a wonderful outcome but a misguided strategy.

Therefore, two things happen. Frustration builds as you realize that you cannot think exclusively positive thoughts. This recognition can lead to an identity crisis if you're not careful. Thinking that you're inadequate or in some way not yet good enough. The other thing that tends to happen is that you exhaust yourself converting every negative thought to a positive one. To do this converting all day every day, is extremely tiring and ultimately futile.

The Death of Positive Thinking

You have no more control over your thoughts than you have control over the lottery numbers. But, what you DO with those thoughts is entirely within your control. You can obsess and stress over them, or you can notice them and go about your life. As your understanding of the thought-feeling system, the nature of thought, and the influence of state of mind expands, you will naturally drop positive thinking as a strategy. Why? Because it will no longer make sense. Adding more thinking to the system always takes you further away from clarity and well-being. In short, it lowers performance.

Negative thoughts are not indicative of what you are observing. They are indicative of the state of mind through which you are making the observations.

The solution, then, is quite simple. When you have negative thoughts, let them pass harmlessly and continue to go about your business. When you have positive thoughts, enjoy them.

Your thoughts do not have to interrupt your life.

For example, if you are an aspiring author, you can continue to write even when you're thinking no one will want to read your work. As long as you don't grab the thought and cling on like a pit bull, it will eventually leave as quietly as a well-mannered dinner guest. And that, my friends, is positively wonderful news!

Coming Up ...

What would your life be like if you didn't have any problems? In the next chapter, we will take an honest look at the problems that most of us spend an enormous amount of time, energy, and resources trying to solve, and how to put an end to them once and for all.

Freedom Inquiry

How much more energy would you have if you no longer had to control and police your every thought? What would you love to do with this newly-found energy?

Chapter 15

Eliminate Problems
Forever

Is it really possible to eliminate problems forever? I say, "Absolutely!" because problems don't really exist. Let me ask you this. Can you bring me a problem in a wheelbarrow? Can you observe a problem with binoculars? Can you take a photograph of one? Can you mail a problem to your best friend? Of course you can't.

Built into the word "problem" is the notion that something has happened that shouldn't have or something hasn't happened that should have. It could be a situation or circumstance you don't like, something someone said that you don't agree with, or even a thought you had; and now it feels like you have a problem. Just because it *feels* like you have a problem doesn't mean you actually have one.

When it feels like you have a problem, you have innocently fallen victim to the illusion ... **"If it didn't happen, I wouldn't feel this way."** That sounds perfectly reasonable, and almost everyone would agree with you.

But just because something has happened doesn't mean that you have a problem. If your mind couldn't create the thought that you had a problem, then you wouldn't have one. Another person presented with the same circumstance may not perceive themselves as having a problem, so it is NOT the circumstance that created the problem.

Circumstances are just circumstances until you interpret them. Problems are a creation of the mind. In other words, problems are thoughts in disguise. Your state of mind in the moment is the determining factor as to whether you think you have a problem. Problems look real to the mind that created it, and that is the dilemma. What enables you to see past the illusion is understanding this truth ...

All problems are just an investment in a random thought without considering the state of mind through which the thought is being viewed.

When it looks like you have a problem, don't look to your circumstances for the solution, look inward to your state of mind. Inevitably, you will find an unproductive state of mind creating the illusion of a problem. Your feelings of stress, anger, overwhelm, worry, and consternation let you know. When you stop dwelling on the problem-oriented thoughts, the problem will simply cease to exist.

Let Your Frequency Adjust

It might seem that the best way to eliminate problems is to make a conscious, empowered choice to avoid the "Problems Frequency." Not like some misguided corporate initiative where every time someone says the word "problem", you immediately form a circle, hold hands, sing "Kumbaya", and replace it with the word, "opportunity."

But developing a habit of seeing differently. Purposely looking at problems as challenges or hurdles to be negotiated. Asking yourself powerful questions such as:

- How can I see this differently?

- If what I'm perceiving is a hurdle, how might I get around it?

- What is this challenge here to teach me?

- What thought am I believing that makes this look like a problem?

- How might that thought not be true?

Imagine you are running an obstacle course. You are presented with a series of challenges and hurdles. They can be handled in a variety of creative ways. You can jump over them, climb over them, run through them, or go around them. It would seem like a good idea to exert will and self-discipline to develop this "muscle," wouldn't it?

Here's the problem with cultivating a habit of focusing on the "positive side" of problems. It requires more thinking in order to do it. Anytime you add more thinking, you lower performance and take yourself further away from the clarity that would set you free. What makes this seem like a good idea in the first place is a misunderstanding. It is a state-of-mind problem not a content-of-thinking problem.

When you understand the role state of mind plays in your interpretation of thought, it won't make sense to interfere with the process.

Remember, new thoughts are always flowing through the system, and your state of mind is always trending to well being and clarity. Any interference on your part only contaminates the system.

When your state of mind is unproductive, applying discipline and cultivating positive-thinking habits rarely work. They take you further from well-being. When your state of mind is productive, you will naturally see problems as challenges and hurdles to navigate. You will naturally ask yourself powerful questions. Your access to creative solutions in that state will minimize the need for unproductive thinking that inevitably lowers performance.

Simply put -- **you don't need to adjust your frequency because the system is designed to do it for you.**

What If It's a Real Problem?

Real problems, i.e. logistics, tend to have solutions. Thought-created problems do not.

Real problems, if ignored, tend to get worse. Thought-created problems, if ignored, tend to resolve themselves; after all, they were never real to begin with.

• If you cut your leg, you clean and bandage the wound.

• If your service engine light comes on, you take your car to the dealer.
• If your bathroom faucet is leaking, you phone a plumber.

• If armadillos take up residence under your house, you call a specialist to humanely trap and relocate them. (Hey, I'm not making that one up. It really happened!)

This is all fairly straightforward, and that is the key. **When it's not straightforward, you are almost always dealing with an imaginary problem -- a problem that you have created with your thinking.**

Most problems are figments of the imagination that created them.

Once you see that, there is really nothing to do other than stop trying to figure it out, and wait for your thinking to shift on its own.

A Business Dilemma

Amy is a professional photographer with her own portrait and wedding studio. She operates in a small town in the Pacific Northwest. Her big problem right now is that she has a to-do list a mile long.

She has post-production work on two weddings and a portrait session, she has brochures to distribute around town, she has several blog posts to write, over 100 emails to deal with, and a half dozen phone calls to return. Her inner dialogue goes something like this:

"I'm too busy doing administrative tasks. I really need to hire some part-time help and outsource some of this post-production work. But I don't have enough revenue to justify those expenses.

What I really need is more clients. To get more clients I need to boost my marketing, but I've already maxed out my marketing budget for the year. Of course, I could raise my prices but in this town that would be suicide; people here don't have that kind of money.

I wonder if I'll ever make my dreams come true. I used to love photography. Now, I'm not doing nearly enough of it. All this tedious work. I need some chocolate."

Let's contrast this with a very different response to the perceived problem:

Amy looks at her to-do list and realizes (thinks) she has much more to do than one person can reasonably do. Suddenly, she feels overwhelmed. When she recognizes the feeling of overwhelm as a signal that her thinking is muddled, she has an insight to take a walk outside.

When she gets back, she feels more energized and makes some important decisions. First, she decides to outsource her post-production work for weddings because she no longer enjoys it, and it takes far too much of her time. She checks a couple of websites and makes a phone call. Within 30 minutes, she identifies the firm to use for post-production and sends them the image files from both weddings.

Then, she decides to hire a high school student to distribute the flyers for her and places an ad on Craigslist.com. She schedules an appointment with herself to brainstorm low-cost marketing strategies and emails five of her colleagues to see if they would like to join the brainstorming session over Skype.

She takes a quick look at the blog posts and decides that only one is critical, so she completes that one in twenty minutes. Then, she turns to email with a ruthless attitude. She deletes everything that is not important, leaving her with only 24 to respond to. She sets a timer for 30 minutes and decides that she will answer as many as she can and leave the rest for tomorrow. She answers 17, leaving her with only 7.

She gets up and goes for another walk to stretch her legs. When she gets back, she returns the phone calls and declares herself done for the day. She packs up her laptop so she can edit the portrait images at home later. On the way home, she has another insight. She decides to raise her prices modestly and get regular help on the tedious tasks she does not enjoy.

She makes a business decision to spend the majority of her time marketing, shooting, and speaking with clients and potential marketing partners. She is excited about the future.

Whether it's the world of business, relationships, career, or any other aspect of life, problems are birthed and destroyed in your own mind. Your understanding of the link between state of mind and perception enables your thinking to shift naturally. And that understanding is all it takes for you to see things differently, and watch your problems disappear.

Coming Up ...

Have you bought into the popular notion that in order to be successful, you must believe in yourself first? In the next chapter, you'll learn why belief is not the panacea it's made out to be, and how you can use an approach more powerful than belief to get where you want to go.

Freedom Inquiry

What problem are you currently struggling with that you now see is not a real problem? What would be the benefit of no longer thinking about this perceived problem?

Chapter 16

Don't Start Believin'[10]

So often you hear about the importance of believing in yourself, whether it's in the world of sports, at work, or in business. Those who succeed talk about self-belief as being critical to the results they enjoy.

We have been trained to believe in BELIEF. After all, what you believe is super important isn't it?

- Don't you need to believe that you can be successful?
- Don't you need to believe that you deserve the big promotion?
- Don't you need to believe that you are the better athlete?
- Don't you need to believe that you have what it takes to be wealthy?

The importance of what you believe is based on an important assumption -- that there are really two choices -- either you believe in yourself or you don't. Those are the two choices: Belief or Lack of Belief.

Clearly, it is much better to believe in yourself than not to. Believing in yourself is more optimistic, more relaxed, more focused on the present, and more creative. BUT there's a problem with what you believe even if it is positive. How you arrive at what you believe is very often based on what happens outside of you, things often beyond your control.

Sure, your belief level is high when:

- You're winning
- Things are going well
- You're getting good results
- You're getting positive feedback from upper management
- You're generating new business
- Your portfolio is growing

That's all well and good until things begin to shift. When your thoughts look like reality, even if they portray you as a winner, you will eventually see yourself as a loser when what you observe changes enough. As long as it seems like the content of your thoughts matters, then you are limited.

Why? Because "What You Believe" is a slippery slope; it is one end of a pendulum. No matter how long the pendulum is or how slowly it swings, eventually it heads in the other direction.

Belief is a poor substitute for knowing.

Whether you believe you're invincible or you believe you're a loser, it's not so much about whether you're right or not, it's about how convinced you are that your opinion matters.

I worked with a very successful businesswoman named Maureen whose career has been triumphant by any standards. The one thing that has troubled her most is the inner doubts about her aptitude as a mom. In short, she was convinced that she was a failure as a mom.

At one point, she was really clashing with her teenage children. After every negative encounter, the thoughts would come rushing back, "I must not be a very good mom." What followed was a sense of sadness that for all her accomplishments, she wasn't able to connect with her children, something she dearly wanted to do.

As we worked together, and she began to gain some separation from her thinking and start to see it for what it was, she began to relax into life for the first time. Both at work and at home, things that once ate at her for days now rolled off her back. She began to appreciate so much more.

As Maureen's demeanor shifted, she became less judgmental. She saw less need to control her teenagers, her husband, or even her own thinking. Rather than shift her behavior in spite of a low state of mind (which wouldn't be sustainable), her behavior shifted naturally as she saw life differently (a permanent shift).

It wasn't long before her daughter said something that normally would've upset her. She could feel her anger and judgment rising up. But this time something was different. She noticed the emotions but didn't act on them. Even though her daughter continued with what looked like an attempt to draw her into an argument, Maureen didn't bite.

Her understanding helped her recognize "the devil inside." She knew the anger she was feeling wasn't because of her daughter. It was just some meaningless thoughts flavored by her own angered state of mind.

That space enabled her to see something subtle yet profoundly different. She saw the innocence of her daughter for the first time in a long time. She could see that her daughter's behavior had nothing to do with her. Her daughter's state of mind was coloring her thinking. She was acting out based on that. She didn't know any better.

Maureen was able to put her arm around her daughter and ask her lovingly what was wrong. And after consoling her for a bit while her daughter got her emotions out, they were able to talk honestly and openly.

From that point forward their relationship transformed. Feeling safer, her daughter began confiding in her more and more. And while things weren't always perfect after that, Maureen no longer saw herself as a bad mom. In fact, she knew beyond a shadow of a doubt that she'd done the best she could, and she was okay with that.

The rest of her life began to shift as she rolled with the tide much more smoothly. It wasn't that her circumstances suddenly improved, it was that she was tapped into her innate capacity to handle anything with grace.

One thing that no one talks about is that what you believe is not really the issue. **It's THAT you believe that is the issue.**

People spend so much time trying to figure out how to believe in themselves, why they don't, what's wrong with them. They work on confidence, self-esteem. They visualize, create vision boards, write affirmations. **All this because they believe that what you believe matters.**

Hey, I get it. Everybody is always saying things like, "If you don't believe in yourself, no one else will." We have been seduced into thinking that belief matters. So we do things to build up our self-belief. And we struggle mightily when we realize we don't have it. That is both counter-productive and completely unnecessary.

If you can see that no single thought is relevant or meaningful until you decide that it is, you are on the brink of freedom. If you didn't believe in your thoughts of excellence or failure, but instead just showed up and worked or competed to the best of your ability with full focus and commitment to the task at hand, you would experience a dramatic difference in your results and how you experience life.

I'm not endorsing apathy here. What I'm saying is **you will enjoy life more and produce better results when there is less on your mind.**

What is holding you back is not what you believe. If you want to joyfully increase your results, performance, and fulfillment, don't start believin'!

Don't believe...

- Your thoughts and judgments are significant.
- What you believe matters.
- Without belief, you can't succeed.
- More or better thinking will help you feel happier or perform better.

Believing is another form of personal thinking, and more thinking is what takes you out of your peak performance state. It's what takes you away from creating the life you want. If you didn't view thoughts as something to believe in (or not), but as things that show up in your consciousness somewhat randomly, then you could ignore them and put your attention on creating success instead.

When there is nothing much on your mind, a natural belief, a knowing, arises. A knowing that you are capable and prepared. A knowing that you can handle any hand you're dealt. Nothing wrong with that. You just have to be aware that the thinking that comes up is not something to get caught up in - good or bad.

The truth is -- you don't need to believe anything to be happy and produce amazing results. You just have to be willing to act with the freedom of not knowing what will happen, and the childlike curiosity to find out for yourself.

Freedom Inquiry

How would your actions change and your results improve if you began with the notion that whatever you happen to believe right now is 100% irrelevant?

What's Next?

On a recent birding trip to Cape May, New Jersey, my family and I had a clear mission -- we wanted to see as many new species of birds as possible. The good news was that our internet research confirmed that there were numerous uncommon birds in the area. The only dilemma was we didn't know the area that well, and given the size of the area and the birds we were seeking, it was a bit like searching for a needle in a haystack.

We opted to head first to Cape May State Park and encountered a group of birders in the parking lot with what appeared to be an experienced leader. We asked him if they had any noteworthy sightings, and sure enough, he told us they had just observed two sea ducks, a Common Eider and a King Eider, just offshore.

He told us to look straight out from the old World War II concrete bunker and toward St. Mary's Jetty. That was enough to get us started. When we arrived at the bunker, there were no birds visible on the water. It then occurred to me that I had no idea where St. Mary's Jetty was. Alas, I scanned with my binoculars and saw a group of birds fly and land on the water a few hundred yards away.

We walked down the beach to get close enough for a good view in our spotting scope and saw a group of Brants on the water. This was a lifer for all three of us! We were thrilled!

As a side note, serious birders keep a list of all the birds they have seen in the wild; this is known as a life list. When a birder sees a species for the first time in the wild, it's called a lifer. If you want to see a birder get excited, suggest the possibility of a lifer. I know it sounds nuts, but it's true.

Then we noticed a couple looking at something else through a scope a bit further down the beach, so we decided to go check it out. We got close enough to the couple to see the two shapes on the water that they were observing, and focused our scope in the birds' direction. Bingo! The Common and King Eider. Two more beautiful birds and lifers at that!

There was not much else on the water so we headed back to our car, when we encountered the helpful group of birders still milling about. We stopped to thank the leader and as we were talking, he told us about a Western Grebe that had been reported in Cape May Harbor. This was a spectacular bird, and one we really wanted to see.

In general, it didn't belong in the east so this was a rare opportunity for us. We knew that the bird had been seen in the harbor, but really had no clue where to look. The harbor was massive, and the grebe could have been anywhere. But again we were in luck.

Our new birding friends pointed us in the right direction. They suggested that we park at the Cape May Nature Center, walk across the street, and look near a buoy that would be fifty yards offshore and just left of a moored sailboat sitting in the harbor.

They also mentioned that we might be able to see a Horned Grebe in Sunset Lake, as they had seen one there earlier. This would be a life bird for my wife, and my son and I would certainly welcome the chance to get a closer look at a bird we had only seen once at a great distance.

Within an hour of that brief conversation with the birders at Cape May State Park, we had added both the Western and Horned Grebe to our lists. It was exhilarating, and the whole experience illustrates an incredibly important point, and one that I am passionate about.

If there is something you wish to experience or accomplish in life, there are times when having a mentor or an experienced guide makes a world of difference. Had we not gotten the sage advice from the experienced Cape May birder, it's quite likely we would not have seen all five of those new species, if any, and it's certain that it would've taken us much, much longer to do it on our own.

There is tremendous value in having a trusted partner to guide you as you navigate your life. That's certainly been my experience. My highest return investments have consistently been hiring coaches to help me get to the next level.

Getting high level coaching has accelerated my growth, dramatically increased my skills, expanded my thinking, and helped me see possibilities I was struggling to see. The reason that productive, rich experiences are the norm for me, while stress and confusion are a rare exception is 100% due to coaching.

That's why I wrote this book. I want to share with you what I've been blessed to learn from amazing mentors, coaches, and teachers in my life. Their inspiration and guidance has helped me find my life's work (something that for a long time didn't seem possible), and to master the skills and understanding that lead to greater fulfillment, satisfaction, and success.

Now I'm here to help speed up your learning curve, to help you have new insights, and continually point you back to the source of your greatness -- inside you. That's the most powerful, sustainable way. When you're in a productive, clear state of mind, you know what's best for you. You know what to do.

I'm committed to the difference you want to make in the world, your well-being, and your desire to be completely and totally free. Know this, my understanding continues to deepen each and every day and, if you're willing to look beyond the intellect to something deeper, so will yours.

If you've enjoyed reading *How Much Freedom Can You Stand*, I'd like to invite you to do two things. First, I'd love for you to get Book 2 in this series, *How Much Freedom Are You Missing*. The second installment shatters the pervasive myths about what really leads to high levels of success.

If you've attributed your success to your ability to set achievable goals, exude confidence, thrive under pressure, stay mentally tough, and stick to your commitments, this is a must-read.

There's a much simpler way to create extraordinary levels of success. Whether you're hungry for new levels of achievement or eager to finally break through, *How Much Freedom Are You Missing* is your ultimate guide to overcoming any challenge... the stress-free way. You can get it at **www.freedomfirstliving.com/books**.

The second thing I'd love for you to do is join the global movement of women entrepreneurs and business leaders (yes, men are welcome, too) who are creating extraordinary results the stress-free way. Hop over to **www.freedomfirstliving.com/freedom** and join the conversation.

This community has one and only one purpose -- to help women like you have fun making the impact you want to make in the world and do it without stress, pressure, and an ever-growing list of things to do -- in short, to finally be free.

The foundation for all greatness is a free mind.

You matter. Your life matters. And your freedom matters.

No matter where you are right now in your life, just know this. You're always only one thought away from freedom. You're much closer to the life you've always dreamt about than you realize. If there is anything I can do to assist you, please contact me. I'm always happy to speak with anyone who reaches out.

To your freedom and success!
Tim

The Freedom Folio
More Stress-Free Ways
to Live the Life You Really Want

Are you ready for even more freedom, simplicity, and success than ever before? Then, *The Freedom Folio* is just what you need.

This free bonus to the *How Much Freedom* series is packed full of insights designed to eliminate any and every last thread of limitation in your life and catapult you to the ultimate freedom!

You'll get 11 exclusive, unpublished chapters that aren't available anywhere else, including:

- Are You All Tapped Out?: Why Stress Management Techniques Rob You of Freedom

- On Second Thought: Make Great Decisions Every Time

- The Top 5 Reasons People Procrastinate and Why You'll Never Have to Again

- It's Hard to Love Something You Hate: The Stress-Free Way to Discover Your Passion

- Too Stressed to De-stress: The Simple Way to Be Free From Stress Forever

Go to **www.freedomfirstliving.com/freedomfolio** to get your copy today. It'll rock your world, Freedom First Style!

Endnotes

1. The song, *Born Free*, is the title track off the eighth studio album of American musician, Kid Rock, released in November 2010.
2. Sydney Banks is a Scottish-born author, philosopher, and lecturer. In 1973, he came to a profound understanding of the principles behind the human experience that he later formulated into the Three Principles of Mind, Consciousness, and Thought.
3. The song, *Devil Inside*, was the third track from the 1987 album, *Kick*, by Australian band, INXS. It reached #2 on the U.S. Billboard Hot 100.
4. This is a reference to the 2006 film, *The Devil Wears Prada*, starring Meryl Streep based on the popular 2003 novel by Lauren Weisberger.
5. This is a reference to a lyric from the title track to the album, *Hotel California*, released by the rock band, the Eagles, in December 1976.
6. "One Bad Apple" is a #1 single released by The Osmonds in 1970.
7. This is a reference to a lyric from the 1970 #1 hit song, "ABC," by the Jackson 5.
8. This story is inspired by a fictional account I first heard told by Greg Baer, M.D. during a radio interview where a person's perspective shifts immediately when they discover that rudeness is actually a person in distress.
9. I first learned this exercise from Jen Louden, whose work I deeply admire. When I saw how much of my life was not "really true," I was astonished.
10. The title is a a a twist on the song, *Don't Stop Believin'*, which was a #9 hit by the American rock band Journey from their 1981 album, *Escape*.
11. Source, *Left to Tell: Discovering God Amidst the Rwandan Holocaust*, the autobiography written by Immaculée Ilibigiza and published by Hay House in 2006.
12. Source, Associated Press story filed in Key West, FL on September 2, 2013.

Declare Your Independence!

Live the Freedom First Lifestyle

IF YOU WANT TO SOAR, YOU NEED FREEDOM FIRST!

If you're like most people who read books like this, you have insights, you're excited about the possibilities, and you're ready to live with an amazing new sense of freedom!

Then life intervenes. With the best intentions and will in the world, you find yourself slipping into old patterns and wondering what's wrong. Maybe not all the time but more often than you'd like.

I understand. The good news is there's nothing wrong with you, and there is a solution. Stay in the conversation! The Freedom First Living conversation that is.

That's why I created the Freedom First Living blog -- to share weekly insights with you. Week by week, you'll learn how to create a wildly successful business on your own terms. Happiness, freedom, creativity, relaxed productivity, and the ability to navigate even the most challenging circumstances will be your new normal.

Because the focus is on helping you grow a sustainable, highly profitable business and have a wonderful life too, you'll get insights on how to:

- Dramatically increase sales
- Gracefully address client's objections,
- Get more done in less time (without more things to learn or do)
- Have fun parenting, even with your surly teenager
- Experience more love and less discord in your marriage

...and much, much more!

Over time the possibilities you've envisioned will become your reality. That's my commitment to you. Join the Freedom First Living conversation today -- go to **www.freedomfirstliving.com/freedom** to learn more.

Succeed With Ease

Extraordinary Business Results the Stress-Free Way

Seems everybody's got a new training these days. Each promising to help you reach extraordinary new heights of success. Yet, almost every single one inadvertently points you in the wrong direction.

It's one thing to succeed by pushing harder, managing stress, and willing your way to victory. But if you're like most people, you've discovered that doesn't always work, and even if it does, the toll it takes is a heavy one.

That's not the kind of success I'm guessing you're interested in. I'm guessing you want rich relationships, peace of mind, and fulfilling, highly profitable work that excites and challenges you.

You want plenty of free time to spend with your spouse and kids. You want vibrant health and the freedom to travel and work from wherever you want whenever you feel like it. You want to live life on your terms.

Succeed with Ease -- The Course will show you how. Not by filling your head with more information or mindset tricks. By teaching you the most powerful, least stressful way to perform your best and create the life you've always wanted.

WARNING -- This is NOT a typical success course. What you'll learn here isn't being taught by other experts. This isn't about personal development (although you'll be happier and more relaxed by the end of the course).

It's like learning how a magician accomplishes a jaw-dropping illusion. You'll finally learn what's really going on when people succeed so you can do the same. It's what catapulted me from clients paying me $150/month to $30,000/year, almost overnight.

One more word of caution -- what you learn may lead to meaningful success in ALL areas of your life. Without stress. Without overwhelm. Without wasting time, energy, or money.

To learn more, go to **www.freedomfirstliving.com/courses**.

Additional Resources

Tim Chaney's Website
www.freedomfirstliving.com

The place to read Tim's weekly blog to learn more stress-free ways to succeed in business and life on your own terms.

Private Consulting
www.freedomfirstliving.com/services

From exclusive VIP days to year-long business and personal transformations, Tim works privately with clients to help them achieve extraordinary results the Freedom First way. If you're ready to experience far less stress, way more freedom, and make way more money doing what you love, submit an application for a complimentary Freedom First Living Strategy Session with Tim at **www.freedomfirstliving.com/services**.

Speaking
www.freedomfirstliving.com/speaking

Need a compelling speaker for your next event? Tim Chaney delivers. Rather than motivate your group for a few hours or a few days, Tim's message will leave them forever changed. Tim's simple, fun, no-nonsense style will be a breath of fresh air that participants will benefit from long after his talk is over. To book Tim for your next event or conference, email **monica@freedomfirstliving.com**.

Executive Coaching/Corporate Training
www.freedomfirstliving.com/speaking

Are you a leader in a fast-growing, dynamic company ready to take your business to the next level? Do you want to build a fun, innovative work culture that constantly raises the bar on what's possible?

No matter how smart and talented your people are or how unique your product or service is, there are hidden factors that can adversely affect your company's performance. With an understanding of how these factors are impacting their performance, you will be equipped to lead your people to consistently perform up to, and often beyond, their capabilities.

Working closely with Tim, you'll learn what these hidden factors are and exactly how you can leverage them so you and your team:

- Innovate more
- Get more done with less resources
- Respond powerfully to change and setbacks
- Work more collaboratively and compassionately to deliver results that are greater than the sum of the individual contributions
- Sell more effectively
- Do more great work
- Thrive in any economy
- Solve the most challenging, complex problems easily
- Astonish your clients with a consistently high level of service
- Retain your best people

Working with Tim is extremely high ROI -- it's the training that will maximize your people's existing skills and future training.

To explore how working with Tim can help you and your organization, email Tim directly at **tim@freedomfirstliving.com** to schedule an exploratory conversation.

Social Media
www.facebook.com/freedomfirstliving
www.pinterest.com/chaneytim
www.twitter.com/timchaney
www.youtube.com/timchaneyTV

Want a daily dose of wisdom, inspiration, and practical advice for living a Freedom First Lifestyle? Want to know the best business books and leading experts worth following? Want to be the first to hear about Tim's upcoming events and programs? Want access to exclusive, private webinars designed to grow your business exponentially? Follow Tim on any of these social media channels and watch your business take off.

Email
tim@freedomfirstliving.com

About the Author

For years, Tim Chaney was on a desperate search to escape a career that just felt wrong - like wearing someone else's shoes. His search for lucrative, passion-filled work seemed like it would never bear fruit until one day, he heard an announcement on a radio show that changed his life forever. And on that day, Tim decided to devote his life to helping people realize their dreams and create meaningful, joy-filled lives.

Now that Tim knew what he wanted to do, he had only one problem. To succeed, he'd have to learn how to sell his services, and he hated to sell! His fear and anxiety around selling seemed insurmountable.

Thanks to some wonderful mentors, Tim had a series of insights that completely transformed his experience of sales. Almost overnight, his individual sales jumped from a few hundred dollars to multiple 5-figures. More importantly, he felt free on the inside, knowing that no matter how long a thought has seemed real to you, you can transcend it in an instant.

Tim's insights were so profound they formed the foundation for all his work. Now Tim teaches women entrepreneurs and business leaders to succeed without stress, pressure, and overwhelm. He helps them consistently produce innovative ideas, take productive action, and gracefully create unprecedented results.

Tim writes a weekly blog on the fun, stress-free way to succeed in business and life. He also speaks to and trains organizations to develop high-performance, high-innovation teams that consistently solve challenging problems with ease. To learn more about how Tim can help you create breakthrough results with ease, visit his website at **www.freedomfirstliving.com**.

Tim is a graduate of the University of Virginia and currently resides in Charlottesville, VA with his beautiful wife and wonderful son. He's a huge baseball fan, an avid birder, and he never turns down a trip to Ben & Jerry's for cookie dough ice cream.

www.ingramcontent.com/pod-product-compliance
Lightning Source LLC
LaVergne TN
LVHW021456080426
835509LV00018B/2300